The Power of Covenant Prayer

Francis Frangipane

CREATION
HOUSE
Orlando, FL

THE POWER OF COVENANT PRAYER by Francis Frangipane
Published by Creation House
Strang Communications Company
600 Rinehart Road
Lake Mary, Florida 32746
Web site: http://www.creationhouse.com

Unless otherwise noted, all Scripture quotations are from
the New American Standard Bible. Copyright © 1960, 1962,
1963, 1968, 1971, 1972, 1973, 1975, 1977 by the Lockman
Foundation. Used by permission.

Scripture quotations marked NKJV are from the New King
James Version of the Bible. Copyright © 1979, 1980, 1982 by
Thomas Nelson, Inc., publishers. Used by permission.

Scripture quotations marked AMP are from the Amplified
Bible. Old Testament copyright © 1965, 1987 by the
Zondervan Corporation. The Amplified New Testament
copyright © 1954, 1958, 1987 by the Lockman Foundation.
Used by permission.

Scripture quotations marked KJV are from the King James
Version of the Bible.

Library of Congress Cataloging-in-Publication Data:
Frangipane, Francis.
  The Power of Covenant Prayer / Francis Frangipane.
    p. cm.
  ISBN: 0-88419-548-1
  1. Spiritual warfare. 2. Witchcraft. I. Title.
BT975.F73 1998
235'.4—dc21   98-3466
                                                       CIP

Portions of the book were previously published as
The Divine Antidote, copyright © 1994.

8 9 0 1 2 3 4 5 BBG 8 7 6 5 4 3 2 1
Printed in the United States of America

Contents

Preface

IN MY BOOK *The Stronghold of God,* we taught that God has a spiritual shelter for His people. Because the theme of that book is somewhat carried over into this book, we recommend that you first become familiar with *The Stronghold of God* before proceeding.

Introduction

A WOMAN FROM another state who had been active in witchcraft gave her life to the Lord, moved to Iowa, and began attending our church. During my initial conversation with her, she told me something remarkable. She said, "You know, when I was into witchcraft, every satanist I knew was daily trying to curse you."

She mentioned that a list of ten Christian leaders had been distributed to satanic covens throughout North America for the purpose of putting curses on those leaders. Because of my work in spiritual warfare and because the Lord was using this ministry to unite Christians in prayer for their cities, I was included on that list.

After our conversation, I called a man who had been nationally known as a leader in the occult but had recently come to Christ. I asked him if it was true that satanists were seeking to put curses upon my life. He said it was true, mentioning that before he became a Christian, he himself participated in the practice. My first response was a mixture of laughter and amazement.

"It is astonishing to me that thousands, perhaps tens of thousands, of satanists are daily cursing me, while I am aware only of the increasing blessings on my life," I said. I wanted to quote Elijah, "Perhaps their god is sleeping or away on a journey." (See 1 Kings 18:27.)

But before I could say another word, he interrupted me and said, "These satanists have tremendous powers. Don't belittle what they can do. It is only because you walk close to the Lord that their curses can't reach you."

"Walking close to the Lord" is the theme of this book; it also provides us with the power of covenant prayer, the weapon we use to combat not only satanic curses, but all of life's ills. I know that because I endeavor to walk near to Jesus, He has sheltered me from the curse of the enemy.

I am not assuming an invulnerability to

satanic attacks, for that would be presumption, not immunity. I know that I have areas in my heart that could leave me exposed to the enemy. As such, I know that my best defense against the devil is to maintain a humble heart before the Lord. While I am aware that every virtue in my life is still growing, I also am aware that God has given me a special grace—preparing my heart for spiritual warfare I know the blessing of the Lord has hedged my soul from the enemy; God's goodness has become a haven for my family, my church, and—to a certain degree—my city.

Additionally, even when the enemy was granted permission to sift my life, God used those times to train my hands for war. Indeed, in the very areas where Satan sought to destroy me, God has now anointed me to teach others how to overcome. The Father has faithfully led me in His triumph in Christ.

My boast is in the Lord, for the power of God's blessing is immeasurably stronger than the assault of Satan's curses. The Lord has faithfully given me His divine antidote to cancel the effects of the enemy. In the midst of great conflicts, the Lord has continually brought my soul into His stronghold. He has impressed upon my heart to teach others also.

—*Francis Frangipane*

Part One:
Prevailing Prayer

For the weapons of our warfare are not carnal, but mighty through God to the pulling down of strongholds.

—2 CORINTHIANS 10:4, KJV

1

Legal Protection

Faith is more than doctrines.

Approximately two thousand years ago, a decree was issued from the judgment seat of God. It provided "legal" protection for the church against the devil. Indeed, when Jesus died for our sins, the "ruler of this world" was judged (John 16:11). Our debts were nailed to Christ's cross and canceled; principalities and powers were disarmed. Because of Jesus, we have a legal right not only to be protected from our enemy but to triumph over him (Col. 2:13–15).

The sacrifice of Christ was so complete and the judicial decision from God against

Satan so decisive that divine protection, enough to cover even the entire church in a city, has been granted. (See Revelation 3:10.) Christ's death is the lawful platform upon which the church rises to do spiritual warfare; His Word is the eternal sword we raise against wickedness. Having said that, we must also acknowledge that the church has only rarely walked in such victory since the first century. Why? The answer is this: To attain the protection of Christ, the church must embrace the intercession of Christ. We must become a house of prayer.

Indeed, church history began with her leadership devoted to the Word of God and to prayer (Acts 2:42; 6:4). Every day the leaders gathered to pray and minister to the Lord (Acts 3:1). In this clarity of vision and simplicity of purpose, the church of Jesus Christ never had greater power or capacity to make true disciples. These men and women revealed the purity of the kingdom of God.

Today, however, our qualifications for church leadership include almost everything but devotion to God's Word and prayer. Leaders are expected to be organizers, counselors, and individuals with winning personalities whose charms alone can draw people.

In Luke 18, Jesus challenges our modern

traditions. He asks, "When the Son of Man comes, will He find faith on the earth?" (v. 8). His question is a warning to Christians who would limit the power of God at the end of the age. Jesus is calling us to resist the downward pull of our traditions; He is asking us individually, "Will I find faith in you?"

Before we respond, let us note that Jesus associates faith with "day-and-night" prayer (Luke 18:7). He is not asking, "Will I find correct doctrines in you?" The Lord's question does not so much concern itself with *right knowledge* as with *right faith*. *What* we believe is important, but *how* we believe is vital in securing the help of God.

Indeed, procuring the supernatural help of God is exactly the point of Jesus' parable in Luke 18. His intent was to show that "at all times" we "ought to pray and not to lose heart" (Luke 18:1). To illustrate the quality of faith He seeks, He followed His admonition with a parable about a certain widow who petitioned a hardened judge for "legal protection" (v. 3). Although the judge was initially unwilling, yet by her "continually coming" (v. 5) she gained what was legally hers.

Jesus concluded by asking: "If an unrighteous judge will respond to a widow's persistence, shall not God avenge quickly

3

His elect, who cry to Him day and night, and will He delay long over them?" Jesus said, "I tell you that He will bring about justice for them speedily." (See Luke 18:1–8.)

UNDERSTANDING GOD'S DELAYS

OUR HEAVENLY JUDGE WILL NOT DELAY LONG OVER His elect, but He will delay. In fact, God's definition of "speedily" and ours are not always synonymous. The Lord incorporates delays into His overall plan: Delays work perseverance in us. So crucial is endurance to our character development that God is willing to delay even important answers to prayer to facilitate our transformation.

Thus, we should not interpret divine delays as signs of divine reluctance. Delays are tools to perfect our faith. Christ is looking to find a tenacity in our faith that prevails in spite of delays and setbacks. He seeks to create a perseverance within us that outlasts the test of time, a resolve that actually grows stronger during delays. When the Father sees this quality of persistence in our faith, it so touches His heart that He grants "legal protection" to His people.

DESPERATION PRODUCES CHANGE

IT IS SIGNIFICANT THAT JESUS COMPARED HIS ELECT

to a widow harassed by an enemy. The image is actually liberating, for we tend to conceptualize the heroes of the faith as David or Joshua type individuals whose successes obscure their humble beginnings But each one of God's servants has, like the widow, a former life that is brimming with excuses and occasions to waver.

Look at the widow: She has legitimate reasons to quit, but instead she prevails. Indeed, she refuses to exempt herself from her high potential simply because of her low estate. She makes no apologies for her lack of finances, knowledge, or charm. Giving herself no reason to fail, she unashamedly plants her case before the judge where she pleads for and receives what is hers: legal protection from her opponent.

How did a common widow gain such strength of character? We can imagine that there must have been a time when, under the relentless pressure of her adversary, she became desperate, and that desperation worked to her advantage. Desperation is God's hammer: It demolishes the stronghold of fear and shatters the chains of our excuses. When desperation exceeds our fears, progress begins.

Today, the force prodding many Christians toward greater unity and prayer has not been the sweetness of fellowship; more often it has been the assault of the enemy. We are in desperate times. When it comes to touching God's heart, other than for a few essential truths, unity of desperation is more crucial than unity of doctrine.

Consider the degree of our national moral decline: In the time it takes to read this chapter, ten babies will be aborted in America. Based on current statistics, this year there will be an estimated thirty-four million crimes committed. Of those, nearly six hundred thousand will be violent crimes, and 72 percent of that number will be against our teenagers. In what place is a teen most frequently assaulted, raped, or murdered today? Most violent acts committed against teens occur in their schools!

GOD'S ELECT

OUR NATION IS SUFFERING FROM A DEEP SOCIAL and moral collapse. If we have ever needed God's anointing it is now, but where are God's elect? Where are the people whom Daniel says "know their God," those who "will display strength and take action" (Dan. 11:32)?

Is there no one divinely empowered who can fell the Goliaths of our age? Perhaps we are looking in the wrong places. Perhaps we need only to look in our bathroom mirror.

If you believe in Jesus and are desperate for God, you qualify as one of God's elect. Remember, in the above parable the widow typifies Christ's chosen.

We have erroneously held that God's chosen will never be assaulted by the adversary, much less driven to desperation and "day-and-night" prayer. But, this desperation is often the very crucible in which the elect of God are forged. Jesus portrays this characteristic metaphorically in the picture of the widow; He reveals the means through which His elect prevail in battle at the end of the age.

When all is said and done, it is also possible that this widow may not have been a singular person but a corporate people— a "widow church"—united in Christ in a singular, desperate prayer for protection against her adversary.

We need the "legal protection" that a national revival provides. But it will not come without unceasing prayer.

You ask, "Where was the prayer behind the Charismatic Renewal?" The Lord spoke to my heart that the Charismatic Renewal was His answer to the cries of a million praying mothers—women who refused to surrender their children to drugs and the devil.

It is our turn to pray. We are the widow

who cannot give herself a reason for failure; God will answer our day-and-night cry. Let us position ourselves at His throne. Certainly, He will grant us legal protection in our cities.

> *Heavenly Father, forgive us for our lack of prayer and for giving ourselves excuses to fail. Lord, we thank You for making us desperate. Help us now to prevail, to attain the "legal protection" You have provided us against our adversary. In Jesus' name. Amen.*

———————————

I kept looking, and that horn was waging war with the saints and overpowering them until the Ancient of Days came, and judgment was passed in favor of the saints of the Highest One, and the time arrived when the saints took possession of the kingdom.

———————————

—DANIEL 7:21–22

2

Day-and-Night
Prayer

God's plan is to make intercessors.

GOD HAS PROVIDED a divine antidote for every ill in the human condition; that remedy is Jesus Christ. When we see a need or a wound in the soul of our communities, we must apply Christ as the cure.

The stronghold that God provides to us as individuals has a divinely inspired, built-in limitation: The Spirit of Christ, which shelters us from the enemy, also makes us vulnerable to the needs of others. As it is written, "If one member suffers, all the members suffer with it" (1 Cor. 12:26). Thus, to perfect love, God unites us to other people; to empower prayer, He allows us to be vicariously identified with the sufferings of those for whom we care. If we cease to love, we will fail to pray. Love is the fuel behind all intercession. Are you weary or vacillating in your prayer life? Remember the love God first gave you, whether it was for your family, church, city, or nation.

Love will identify you with those you love; it will revive your prayer, and prayer will revive your loved ones. Consider Daniel. Daniel loved Israel. He loved the temple. Daniel put on sackcloth and ashes and sought the Lord with prayer and supplication. Although Daniel was not guilty of the sins of Israel, his prayer was an expression of his identification with the nation. He prayed:

> Alas, O Lord, the great and awesome God, who keeps His covenant and lovingkindness for those who love Him and keep His commandments, we have sinned, committed iniquity, acted wickedly, and rebelled, even turning aside from Thy commandments and ordinances.
>
> —DANIEL 9:4–5

Had Daniel sinned? No. But his love and identification with Israel made his repentance legitimate. Additionally, Daniel was faithful in his daily prayer for Israel, having prayed all his life for the restoration of the nation. Consider our own prayers for our nation and for others: After a year or two our faithfulness begins to wane.

Daniel was faithful every day throughout his life! When Darius passed a law forbidding petitions to any god or man other than himself, Daniel was not intimidated. We read:

> Now when Daniel knew that the writing was signed, he went home. And in his upper room, with his windows open toward Jerusalem, he knelt down on his knees three times that day, and prayed and gave thanks before his God, as was his custom since early days.
>
> —DANIEL 6:10, NKJV

Daniel was one of the first exiles from Israel to Babylon. In the terror and trauma of seeing one's society destroyed and its survivors enslaved and exiled, we can imagine that Daniel's parents had firmly planted in his young heart Solomon's prayer, which embodied God's requirements for restoration:

> When Thy people Israel are defeated before an enemy, because they have sinned against Thee, if they turn to

> Thee again and confess Thy name and
> pray and make supplication to Thee in
> this house, then hear Thou in heaven,
> and forgive the sin of Thy people
> Israel, and bring them back to the land
> which Thou didst give to their fathers.
> —1 KINGS 8:33–34

Thus, Daniel prayed three times a day, every day, since his earliest years. He continued in prayer for nearly seventy years, until the time Jeremiah's prophecy came to pass! You see, the work of God takes time. How long should we pray? We pray as long as it takes. Consider Anna, who ministered to the Lord in prayer and fasting in the temple for approximately sixty years, crying out to God until He sent the Messiah. Or Cornelius, whose "prayers and alms . . . ascended as a memorial before God" (Acts 10:4).

We do not understand the responsibility and privilege God places upon a person who continues in faithful prayer. What sustained these champions of prayer? They loved God and loved the people of God.

COSTLY LESSONS

WHILE THE WORK OF REVIVAL IS OFTEN INITIATED through the love and intercession of one person, there is a time when the prayer burden must be picked up and shared by many. It is not enough that God graces one individual to become a man or woman of prayer; the Lord seeks to make His church a house of prayer.

One way or another the plan of God is to make intercessors of us all. We can learn the indispensable priority of prayer directly from God's Word. We can also learn of the need to pray from the victories or mistakes of others. Or, we can learn of the necessity of prayer the hard way: We can fail to pray and let the consequences teach us. For some, these will be costly lessons. And we will not be able to blame the devil if the real culprit was our neglect of prayer. In extreme cases, the Lord will actually allow tragedy to reinforce the urgency and priority of prayer.

The following incident from the Book of Acts underscores the need to keep our prayer life strong and sensitive to changes in our spiritual battles. The story also reveals that tremendous power is released when the whole church in a city prays.

Of all Jesus' followers, three were considered the "inner circle": Peter, James, and John. Yet, Luke tells us of a terrible event in the life of the early Christians: Herod executed the apostle James. Until that time the leaders of the church walked in spiritual protection. However, they failed to discern that the intensity of satanic assault had escalated. As a result, James, an apostle who stood with Christ on the Mount of Transfiguration, was beheaded.

The appalling murder of James shocked the church. How was it that this anointed apostle died so prematurely? Where was God's protection? Perhaps this is the answer: The Lord suppressed His *sovereign protection* that He might bring the church into *intercessory protection*.

The death of James pleased the Jews, so Herod imprisoned Peter also, intending to kill him after the Feast of Unleavened Bread. At this point, the Scripture says, "Peter was therefore kept in prison, but constant prayer was offered to God for him by the church" (Acts 12:5, NKJV). The New International Version says the church was praying "earnestly"; the New American Standard Bible tells us that the church was praying "fervently." Earnest, fervent, constant prayer was made for Peter by the entire church in Jerusalem!

The outcome of this aggressive intercession was that Peter was supernaturally delivered, the guards who held Peter were executed, and a short time later Herod himself was struck down by an angel of the Lord. When the entire citywide church engaged in continual day-and-night prayer,

God granted deliverance!

In the many years I have served the Lord, I have known individuals, prayer groups, and even denominations that have embraced varying degrees of twenty-four-hour prayer. I have participated with prayer chains and prayer vigils. But I have yet to see an entire, citywide Christian community put aside minor doctrinal differences and take God's promise seriously.

When the local churches in a community truly become a house united in prayer, God will begin to guide the entire church into the shelter of His protection. And, according to Jesus, "He will bring about justice for them speedily" (Luke 18:8).

> *Lord God, restore us to Your love. Your Word says that love never fails. Master, we know that we have failed often; we faint because we lose sight of love. Master, by Your grace, we purpose to identify those people whom we love and then to be faithful in prayer until You touch them. We also purpose to follow Your leading until all the Christians in the city are crying to You in prayer. Help us, Father, to discern the priority of prayer. In Jesus' name. Amen.*

"For I know the plans that I have for you," declares the Lord, "plans for welfare and not for calamity to give you a future and a hope. Then you will call upon Me and come and pray to Me, and I will listen to you. And you will seek Me and find Me, when you search for Me with all your heart. And I will be found by you," declares the Lord.

—JEREMIAH 29:11–14

3

Repentance
Precedes Revival

We must want deliverance, not just relief.

A TRUE REVIVAL DOES not just happen. There are conditions that must reside in the human heart before the Lord visits His people.

Too often, ministries today seek to deliver people who are unwilling to repent of sins, who have not cried in their hearts to God for help. The effect is that those prayed for may receive limited relief, but they soon fall back into sin and oppression. The key to successful deliverance is to discern if an individual is ready and willing to be released before we minister deliverance. Is he repentant? Has he put away his idols? Is his heart truly turning toward God?

God's pattern for us as individuals is also His pattern for the church and the city. Just as the Lord did not deliver us until we cried for help, so the war for our churches and cities will not be won until a significant number of us are crying to God in prayer. Christ's purpose in bringing the citywide church to prayer is to provide the proper heart attitudes to which the Almighty can respond. Without the substructure of prayer and crying before God, deliverance, "binding and loosing," and other forms of spiritual warfare are significantly limited. *Deliverance,* according to Scripture, is the last stage of a process that began when a person's abhorrence for his present condition led him to cry to God for help.

THE DELIVERERS

THE OLD TESTAMENT REVEALS GOD'S PATTERN for deliverance and revival: In answer to the prayers and sufferings of His people, the Lord raised up deliverers. They were individuals who were anointed and empowered by God to defeat Israel's oppressors.

It is important to note that the effectiveness of these deliverers was never based upon their own worthiness or credentials. While they were uniquely sent by God, their arrival was synchronized with Israel's repentance. No repentance; no deliverance. As Israel cried out to God, the deliverers were commissioned and anointed with the power of the Holy Spirit.

The essence of this Old Testament pattern for renewal can be applied to us in our day. We may not see actual "deliverers" as much as we will see revival emerge in those cities where prayer and repentance is deep and widespread.

Again, looking at the Israel model, national sin brought defeat and dominance by foreign powers. With foreign domination came the worship of demons and the complete seduction of Israel's heart by the enemy. As Israel blatantly defied God's laws, so came the economic, cultural, and physical collapse of the nation. Where once the people enjoyed the blessing of God, now despair and misery dwelt upon the land.

It was in this context of suffering, of people genuinely and deeply crying to God, that the Lord raised up deliverers. These individuals led a repentant Israel into victory over their oppressors. As true worship was established, national peace and prosperity followed.

It should be noted that the route to revival was not set according to a timetable; it was not precisely scheduled. No one can forecast how long judgment might last or when repentance has so excavated the heart of sinful man that God is satisfied. This one fact will be true: The time it takes will always be longer than we expect. The determining factor is the acknowledgment of sin and the return to God. Once the nation was securely turned toward God, healing for her land soon followed.

Nehemiah speaks of this pattern of repentance preceding national deliverance. He prayed:

> Therefore Thou didst deliver them into the hand of their oppressors who oppressed them, but when they cried to Thee in the time of their distress, Thou didst hear from heaven, and according to Thy great compassion Thou didst give them deliverers who delivered them from the hand of their oppressors.
>
> —NEHEMIAH 9:27

We must not hurry this process nor be frustrated if our prayers do not immediately activate divine intervention. The Lord is waiting for the nation to break beneath the weight of her rebellion. Yet, in this we should be encouraged: Our intercession is the first fruits of what is destined to become a national response to the Almighty!

There may be, at times, flurries of spiritual activity, but before a national revival will come, there will be a nation crying to God. This period is called "the time of their distress," and it is not consummated in revival until the nation has been crying unto the Lord for a number of years.

MAN'S MISERY, GOD'S HEART

IN THE BOOK OF JUDGES THIS PATTERN OCCURS time and again. While Israel tumbled deeper into sin, God waited for the burden and consequences of Israel's sin to humble the people's souls. He waited to bring them back to Himself.

Yet, the Lord was not aloof from Israel's sorrows. Even when they were in rebellion, He felt their sufferings. When the Lord "could bear the misery of Israel no longer" (Judg. 10:16), He sent them deliverers. The misery and desperation of Israel readied them for God.

We see this pattern in the Lord's encounter with Moses in Exodus. The Redeemer said:

> I have surely seen the affliction of My people who are in Egypt, and have given heed to their cry because of their taskmasters, for I am aware

of their sufferings. So I have come
down to deliver them.
—Exodus 3:7–8

Notice that the Lord saw the affliction of
His people; He heard their cries; He knew
their sufferings. God is never far from the
plight of mankind. In truth, He bears the
misery of our society: Our distresses distress Him; our suffering becomes His sorrow.

Returning to our text in Exodus, observe
also that it was not merely their prayers that
God heard; He heard their cries. It is one
thing to pray about a need, quite another to
weep over it. It is those who mourn whom
God comforts.

The Lord knew their afflictions and their
sufferings. The prayer to which God re-
sponds is a constant cry, often born out of
"afflictions" and "sufferings," as in the former
Soviet Union and parts of Africa and Asia.

Perhaps the Lord has not fully answered
us because our prayers are still comfortably
contained within a schedule. As we stated
earlier, the Charismatic Renewal began with
the constant, "day-and-night" cry of a million
mothers. This was not the result of a mere
hour of prayer; it emerged out of the continual cry of mothers (and fathers) who were
deeply troubled about their children. Their
prayer was not a religious discipline; it was

the heartthrob of their existence. Without the sophisticated machinery of spiritual warfare, the tears and weeping of their unceasing intercession prevailed before God, and He rescued their children.

Perhaps what delays revival in our times is that we are troubled, but we are not afflicted by the conditions of our society; though saddened, we are not yet weeping. It must be acknowledged, however, that a growing number of God's people have truly surrendered to the vulnerability of Christ's compassions. They bear in their intercessions not only the needs of the people but the pain of the people as well. They are laying down their reputations, their jobs, yes, even their lives to see the sins of our society cleansed. Although still a minority, these intercessors carry in their souls the anguish of their cities. They hear the cry of the oppressed; they know the suffering of both the unborn and the born. God is ready to respond to their prayer. Out of the womb of their distress, God shall bring forth deliverance.

The praying church should not limit the length of her dedication to intercession. God is looking for a life of prayer, not just a season. If the duration of time required to bring change can stop us, it is obvious that the preparatory work in our hearts is not deep enough to draw divine intervention.

How does all this relate to revival? Spiritual renewal is the divine antidote for our cities and our nation. It is God's answer to all who cry unceasingly in covenantal prayer to Him for help.

> *Lord, forgive us for wanting relief instead of deliverance, for looking for shortcuts instead of Your perfect will. Master, we know that Your heart cannot refuse the genuine cry of the afflicted, that You cannot long bear the misery of Your people without acting on our behalf.*
>
> *So, we cry to You today! We covenant with You in prayer on behalf of our land. Send the rain of Your presence back to us! Cleanse us from our lusts for comfort and apathy. Bring us to the place where You can honor Your integrity and bring revival to our land! For Your glory we pray. Amen.*

And He said to them, "I was watching Satan fall from heaven like lightning. Behold, I have given you authority to tread upon serpents and scorpions, and over all the power of the enemy, and nothing shall injure you."

—Luke 10:18–19

4

Sent by God

*Our strength is in our commission
from the Lord.*

DELIVERANCE FOR OUR nation is coming, and
we have written about the fundamental
conditions that precipitate revival. However, it is important to identify the nature of
those whom God sends, lest the enemy
plant counterfeit ministries that stall the
move of God. To give us a general over-
view of the spiritual traits the Lord works in
His servant, we will study the life of Gideon.

Let us recall that deliverers were raised
up when evil and oppression covered the
land. Although instrumental in bringing
great light and prosperity to Israel, the ministry of deliverance was always birthed out

of a womb of social darkness and trauma.

"Now it came about when the sons of Israel cried to the LORD on account of Midian, that the LORD sent a prophet" (Judg. 6:7–8). Once again, we see that the future deliverance of Israel began with the sons of Israel crying to the Lord.

The Lord responded to the Jews with a prophetic word. The prophetic anointing does more than teach; it proclaims the intention of God. It also confronts strongholds of sin in the people and prepares society for an outpouring of the Spirit.

In this case, the prophet was not the deliverer; he simply reminded Israel of former deliverances. He reiterated God's command of many generations: "I am the LORD your God; you shall not fear the gods of the Amorites in whose land you live" (v. 10).

The "gods of the Amorites" were the demonic principalities and powers that ruled the countries in Canaan. There is an interaction between the powers of darkness and the sins of a society. When Israel was in obedience to God, the Spirit of God ruled the heavenly places over Israel. When the Jews were in rebellion, the enemy gained control of the nation through the sins of the people. Evil ruled in the spiritual realms over Israel.

The idols erected to these evil spirits

were physical symbols of spiritual bondage. Paul instructs us that when people sacrifice to an idol, "they sacrifice to demons" (1 Cor. 10:20). However, the Lord commanded Israel not to fear these demon gods. The Hebrew word for *fear* means "to reverence; to live in an intellectual or emotional anticipation of harm." We will never be victorious over the enemy if we fear his retaliation.

It must be stated that it is great wisdom not to move presumptuously in spiritual warfare. No one should be flippant or casual against powers of darkness. Yet, it is a greater error to be afraid of the enemy. Satan does, indeed, have a "right" to occupy the spiritual realms of sin and rebellion. However, we are commanded not to fear the "gods of the Amorites" or, in our case, the "principalities and powers" over our cities.

If a Christian teacher instructs you to fear principalities and powers, you must not fear what he fears. You should respect the power of the enemy, but it is sin to live in fear of these demons. Israel spent forty years in the wilderness because they feared the giants in the land of promise. The Lord has given us authority over all the power of the enemy; He promises, "Nothing shall injure you" (Luke 10:19).

THE MAN IS THE PLAN

THE PROPHET REBUKED ISRAEL FOR FEARING THE gods of the Canaanites. The Lord then set Himself to deliver Israel of fear. God always begins the deliverance of the many with the deliverance of one, and so He sought out Gideon. The angel of the Lord found Gideon hiding from the Midianites. His greeting was astounding, "The LORD is with you, O valiant warrior" (Judg. 6:12). Although the years of preparation might be many, when the Lord unsheathes His sword, He moves quickly.

1. SURPRISED BY THE CALL

God wasted no time in establishing the man of His choosing, calling him by his future identity: valiant warrior. Gideon, no doubt, wondered if he was the valiant warrior to whom the angel spoke. And this is the first aspect of the one whom God intends to use: He is surprised, even shocked, that the Lord has called him! He has no secret wish to be a hero, no hidden ambition for prominence. He is not even a "natural-born" leader.

We might imagine that, in Gideon's fear, he concluded there was another person, a "valiant warrior," near him of whom he was unaware There is a Valiant Warrior in us of whom we too are often unaware. His name is the Lord of Hosts, and greater is He who is in us than he who is in the world.

In this first encounter, Gideon asked the Lord a very legitimate question, "If the LORD is with us, why then has all this happened to us . . . where are all His miracles?" (Judg. 6:13). This is a question that everyone who sincerely seeks the endorsement of God must ask. Why does it seem as though the Lord has abandoned us? We must know why there seems to be a distance between the Lord and our need so that we can repent and be restored.

2. MOVING IN DIVINE AUTHORITY

However, God had not left His people. The question was actually superfluous, for if the Lord initiated this encounter with Gideon, then the time of separation had passed; the time of His visitation was at hand. "And the LORD looked at him and said, 'Go in this your strength and deliver Israel from the hand of Midian. Have I not sent you?'" (v. 14). Gideon was the youngest in his father's house, and his family was the least in Manasseh. What strength had he? How could Gideon deliver Israel? The strength of God's servants is in their commission from the Lord. This is the second aspect of a true servant of God: Having been sent by God, he goes in divine authority.

Let us remember that Jesus gave His disciples the same appointment Gideon received: "As Thou didst send Me into the world, I also have sent them into the world" (John 17:18). The commission of the Lord carries the endorsement of the Lord; He will back with power those whom He sends!

At this point Gideon's eyes were opened, and He saw God. Concerned about his own unworthiness, he cried out, "'Alas, O Lord GOD! For now I have seen the angel of the LORD face to face.' And the LORD said to him, 'Peace to you, do not fear; you shall not die'" (Judges 6:22–23).

3. AT PEACE WITH GOD

Gideon built an altar to the Lord and called it, "The LORD is Peace" (v. 24). No one can truly stand against the enemy if they are unsure of their standing before God. And this is the third aspect of a true servant of God: They have peace with God. Before the Lord sends His servants forth, they must know the power of His blood, the forgiveness of their sins, and their justification by faith. Whenever they look toward heaven, they must know "the LORD is peace."

4. ESTABLISHING DIVINE ORDER

The Lord said, "Pull down the altar of Baal which belongs to your father, and cut down the Asherah that is beside it; and build an altar to the LORD your God on the top of this stronghold in an orderly manner" (Judg. 6:25–26).

The same night that the Lord revealed Himself to Gideon, He sent him to pull down the altar of Baal and also to cut down the Asherah. Now, although the altar to Baal was in the center of town, it belonged to Gideon's father. There is a sequence here worth noting. After the Lord delivered Gideon, He sent him to pull down the strongholds in his family.

This is the fourth aspect of the nature of those whom the Lord sends: They will be anointed to bring order. Generally speaking, that order will begin with their own families. Their homes may not be perfect, but they will be in order. God is very concerned with all the disorder in the church. Those whom God sends will initiate reconciliation and repentance. Because they are individuals who are filled with the grace and truth of Christ, their influence will be greatly respected. But, the process of bringing order will start in the little, nonpublic relationships of their own homes.

We encourage each of you to begin the battle for your city by pulling down the strongholds in your home. Bring your family into prayer and, through prayer, bring healing and order. If you fail in this preparation, the enemy will always have open doors to counterattack and undermine your credibility. (See 1 Timothy 3:5.)

It is important to note that pulling down a stronghold is only half the battle—on that very site we must now build an altar to the Lord. For example, if the stronghold was fear, it must be replaced with an altar of faith. If bitterness existed, love must take its place. On a citywide scale, where perversion once ruled, purity must now reign; where greed was master, generosity must preside. Gideon pulled down his father's altar to Baal, and instead of being welcomed and applauded by the people of Ophah, they came en masse to kill him! The demonic power that ruled the area stirred its captives to fight against the Lord's servant! Gideon's father defended his son, however, and said, "If [Baal] is a god, let him contend for himself" (Judg. 6:31). Be aware: There will be those whose thoughts are so sympathetic with the very evil God has sent you to destroy that they will rise up in defense of the devil! Expect resistance even among God's people!

5. MOBILIZING GOD'S PEOPLE

The Lord used Gideon to mobilize a large army, which the Lord promptly reduced to three hundred soldiers. It is important to note that, in the process of restoration, it will never seem like God has given us enough people or skills to accomplish the task. This lack, however, is met by God. And perhaps this is the last characteristic of those whom God anoints: Having been sent by the Lord with His purpose, they ultimately mobilize God's people to face their enemies and conquer them.

Significantly, Gideon was renamed "Jerub-baal," which meant, "contender with Baal." Whenever there was a name change in the Bible, there was a change of nature as well. Gideon went from being a fearful captive to a fearless warrior.

In summary, in answer to the prayers and cries of His people, a new anointing is coming. Throughout the nations, we see individuals laying down their lives, drawing the church together in repentance and prayer. Out of their surrender, the power is coming to guide both churches and cities toward revival.

They will be sent by God. They will not come to "try" anything; they will come to carry out the expressed purpose of God.

What they decree will come to pass. They will lead a repentant people out of oppression and into God's remedy for their cities—*revival!*

> *Father, draw Your people together to pray, to feel, and to absorb into their souls the desperate condition of their cities. Lord, with Isaiah I say, 'Here am I; send me.' Forgive me for fearing the enemy. Lord, bring Your anointing to Your servants that, through Your power, we might see our nation turned back to You. In Jesus' name. Amen.*

This day I will begin to put the dread and fear of you upon the peoples everywhere under the heavens, who, when they hear the report of you, shall tremble and be in anguish because of you.

—DEUTERONOMY 2:25

5

The Power of
Covenant Prayer

*A covenant with God takes us
further into our goal of Christlikeness.*

IT IS RIGHT to pray for the Lord to bless and protect our lives. However, praying for the blessing and provision of God is not the same as making a covenant with Him. A *covenant* is an altar upon which the Lord and His covenant partner give themselves fully to each other. A covenant relationship with God does not cease once our prayers have been answered. For, in covenant love we mature from simply being "believers" in prayer to becoming living sacrifices given to God's highest plans. By so yielding, He creates within us a life that He can use extraordinarily in the process of divine redemption.

Covenant power is greater than that which comes through prayer alone. Indeed, the effects of a covenant reach far beyond simple faith. Prayer and faith are essentials—they are prerequisites—but not substitutes for covenant power.

Thus, a covenant relationship is a life-long pledge, an unbreakable oath, which God Himself initiates and promises to sustain. Contained within His promise is His unalterable commitment not only to fulfill His highest plan of redemption but also to supply grace and faith to His human counterparts along the way. Together, the all-sufficient God and a believing man accomplish the impossible through their covenant relationship.

POWER RELEASED IN A COVENANT

A COVENANT WITH GOD ACCOMPLISHES TWO interconnected goals. It thrusts us beyond "subjective prayer" (prayer made primarily for our personal needs) and brings us into a deeper commitment to God. Out of greater commitment comes greater grace to accomplish God's redemptive work in the world.

An example of covenant power is seen in ancient Israel during the revival that occurred after Athaliah, an idolatrous Judean queen, was dethroned. Jehoiada, the high priest, looked to God in covenant prayer. We read, "Then Jehoiada made a covenant between the LORD and the king and the people, that they should be the LORD's people" (2 Kings 11:17).

Did not Israel already have a covenant with God through Moses? Yes, but it is a biblical practice that individuals at various times made special covenants with the Almighty. The results of Jehoiada's covenant were that grace came upon the people and they cleansed the land of idolatry.

We read, "So all the people of the land rejoiced and the city was quiet" (v. 20). Jehoiada's covenant brought the nation back to God and ended violence in Jerusalem! Consider also the power released in Hezekiah's covenant with the Lord. The nation of Judah had been fully corrupted by Ahaz, the preceding king. However, Hezekiah began his reign by seeking God's highest favor. He opened the doors of the temple and reconsecrated the priests.

Yet, the purification of priests and buildings would not have brought about revival had not Hezekiah taken one further step. He said, "Now it is in my heart to make a covenant with the LORD God of Israel, that His burning anger may turn away from us" (2 Chron. 29:10). Just eight days after the king made a covenant with the Lord, we read, "Then Hezekiah and all the people rejoiced over what God had prepared for the people, because the thing came about suddenly" (v. 36).

The difference between a long-term struggle to bring a nation around and a speedy recovery was in the power released when the king made a covenant with the Almighty. Keep in mind that Judah was apostate in its religious practices, witchcraft was practiced by the former king, and demonic idols had been placed in the holy of holies. Yet, covenant power triggered a national revival. As Americans, it is vital we remember that our spiritual forefathers were a people who knew and exercised principles of covenant sacrifice. When the Puritans came to this country, they knelt on its shores and made a covenant with God for this land. They dedicated this "new world" to Christ and His kingdom. It is unlikely that the revival of our nation will come without local and national church leaders coming together in a covenant relationship with God for the redemption of America.

COVENANTS WITH GOD FOR OUR TIMES

A PERSONAL COVENANT WITH GOD IS A SERIOUS

commitment, worthy of extended prayer and waiting before God. At Christ's bidding, I have made a covenant with Him to see the body of Christ delivered of carnal divisions and racism so that Christ's prayer in John, chapter 17, may be answered.

What does this covenant signify to me? It means that my life is not my own. It has been absorbed into something much more powerful: the will of God. It also means that when I pray, there is a power attached to my intercession that demands strongholds of religious and cultural pride to fall before God's purposes.

I have also united my life and faith with the covenants of our pilgrim forefathers. Together with a number of other brethren, both locally and nationally, we have made a covenant with the Almighty to see this land restored according to 2 Chronicles 7:14. There will be a time when this nation, like all nations, becomes the kingdom of our Lord and of His Christ (Rev. 11:15). Until then, whether revival comes quickly or we pass through the fires of divine judgments, our lives belong to Christ, not simply to be blessed or made prosperous but to see His highest purposes accomplished in our land.

Not all of us will covenant with God for the nation. Some will unite with the Lord for their families. Others will covenant with God to see abortion ended in their cities. Still others will make a covenant with God for the church, to see the Lord's house built in their cities. Making a covenant with God takes us further into our goal of Christ-likeness. It is the highest relationship we can enjoy with God; it is that which brings Him the most pleasure. To those who covenant with God, He says, "Gather My godly ones to Me, those who have made a covenant with Me by sacrifice" (Ps. 50:5).

Lord, open our hearts to the joy and wonder, the sobriety and fear, of a covenant relationship with You. Lead us, O King, out of the superficial and into the supernatural. Lead us into a covenant with You for our times and nation! In Jesus' name. Amen.

When you see the ark of the covenant of the LORD your God with the Levitical priests carrying it, then you shall set out from your place and go after it…that you may know the way by which you shall go, for you have not passed this way before.

—JOSHUA 3:3–4

6

Covenant Power

The entire history of the conquest of the
Promised Land is a prophecy of the spiritual
conquest of the world through the church
under the leadership of Jesus the Messiah.*

ISRAEL HAD SPENT nearly forty years in the wilderness. Now as they approached the Promised Land, God was about to release a new level of power, one that the Hebrews had never experienced before.

> Then Joshua said to the people, "Consecrate yourselves, for tomorrow the LORD will do wonders among you."
> —JOSHUA 3:5

YOU HAVE NOT PASSED THIS WAY BEFORE

AS SUCCESSFUL AS THEIR TIME OF PREPARATION

was, before they could graduate into new levels of power, God required a new level of consecration. It was time for a fresh surrender to God. Such is the nature of holiness. Israel was holy—not because she kept herself from the world, but because she was set apart unto God and His purposes. All her achievements and failures, sins and virtues were surrendered to the Almighty in preparation for something greater that was to come.

> And it came about at the end of three days that the officers went through the midst of the camp; and they commanded the people, saying, "When you see the ark of the covenant of the LORD your God with the Levitical priests carrying it, then you shall set out from your place and go after it."
> —JOSHUA 3:2–3

It took three days for Israel to consecrate herself unto the Lord. Then Joshua instructed the Hebrews to do one more thing. He said, "When you see the ark of the covenant of the LORD…go after it."

The ark was a gold-covered box forty-five inches long, twenty-seven inches wide, and twenty-seven inches high. It contained Aaron's rod (which had supernaturally budded), a pot of manna (which was supernaturally provided), the two tablets containing the Ten Commandments (which were supernaturally written), as well as the book of the testimony written by Moses defining Israel's covenant with God. The ark was Israel's holy standard. As the priests carried it in sacred procession, it proclaimed boldly and fearfully: Israel's God was a covenant-keeping God and supreme Lord even of the impossible.

Israel as a nation unique among peoples would draw her strength from God and His promises to her. Her victories and success would be immutably bound to her covenant with the almighty God. By following the ark, the Israelites were, in truth, following God into the realm where all things are possible.

Yet *Yahweh* of Israel was a holy God as well. He required that there should be a distance between the people and the priests. "There shall be between you and it a distance of about 2,000 cubits by measure. Do not come near it..." (Josh. 3:4). They were not to relate to the presence of God with familiarity nor approach the promises of God carelessly. In obedient faith and holy fear they were to follow.

In closing, Joshua then explained why they needed to consecrate themselves, focus their attention upon the ark, and abide in the fear of the Lord. He said,

"...that you may know the way by which you shall go, for you have not passed this way before" (Josh. 3:4).

Israel had many spiritual experiences. The people possessed a rich spiritual heritage, and they carried in their bosom the blessing and hope of the patriarchs, their spiritual fathers. Yet, as good as their past had been, God had promised the forefathers something that remained unpossessed. Something new and better awaited the Israelites that would exceed what their forefathers had experienced.

Scriptures tell us that Abraham, Isaac, and Jacob received the promises of God and welcomed them "afar off" (Heb. 11:13, NKJV). Yet, Israel was about to possess the promise. To do so, the people too would have to fully rely upon the covenant promise of God, which was within the sacred ark. In truth, they had not gone this way before.

INSTANT FULFILLMENT OF THE WORD

ISRAEL SPENT FOUR HUNDRED THIRTY YEARS IN Egypt; another forty years ticked by as God transformed them from slaves to sons. All this took time, and they were conditioned by the effects of long periods of discipline and learning. But now the ark of the covenant was going before them, guiding them out

of the wilderness into a new realm that
would produce immediate breakthroughs.

> And it shall come about when the
> soles of the feet of the priests who
> carry the ark of the LORD, the Lord of
> all the earth, shall rest in the waters
> of the Jordan, the waters of the
> Jordan shall be cut off, and the
> waters which are flowing down from
> above shall stand in one heap.
>
> —JOSHUA 3:13

As a foretaste of the new realm of immediate, supernatural breakthroughs, the priests
are required to step into the Jordan. It is
deep. The text tells us that "the Jordan
overflows all its banks all the days of harvest" (v. 15). The river does not gradually
recede as the priests draw near; it has not
dried up overnight from a stiff wind like
the Red Sea experience. It is at flood stage
and remains so until the four priests carrying the covenant step out in it.

Each of the first two priests extend a foot
toward the churning, rushing water. Yet, as
their weight follows the downward motion
of their stride, the Jordan at their right side
instantly stops! The extended foot of each
priest lands solidly on dry ground! It was as
if God were saying, "*Welcome to the realm*

of covenant power, the domain where all things are possible!"

The living God was about to lead them outside of the boundaries of their past experiences and into the fulfillment of His promises. Ahead would be victories and answers to prayer that were nearly instantaneous in nature. Nations would be subdued, and the sun in its course would halt at the voice of a man.

New power and greater revelations of God were at hand for the Hebrews. Their confidence would be born of the same covenant they knew in the wilderness, but they would possess new revelation concerning it: They would know in a deeper way what it truly meant to follow God in the day of His power.

In the wilderness experience, the maturation process extended over a prolonged period of time. Indeed, it takes time to become truly obedient in both spirit and deed. The Lord must deliver His people from the false gods of ambition and fear, jealousy and rebellion, murmuring, complaining, and unbelief. Yet, we can be conditioned to expect delays and extended time between our prayers and God's answer. Once true obedience was established, what the Lord would do with the Israelites would, for the most part, occur swiftly.

Note the obedient faith of the priests as they walked toward the dangerous and turbulent water. These were not the same, murmuring Hebrews whose kinsmen died in the wilderness. They did not reason within themselves until they were so full of doubt and fear they were paralyzed. They understood what it meant to rely fearlessly upon the covenant power of God.

Likewise, the next phase of God's will for the church will soon unfold. However, God has not given us a promised land; His holy pledge to us is the nature of Christ and the power of His kingdom to transform our world. The years of preparation are coming to an end. Let us too consecrate ourselves for the new breakthroughs that are at hand. For we too have not gone this way before.

*New American Bible; introduction to the Book of Joshua

His divine power has granted to us everything pertaining to life and godliness, through the true knowledge of Him who called us by His own glory and excellence.

—2 PETER 1:3

7

Every Blessing

The door to the realm where all things are possible is swinging open before us!

THE SON OF God spent thirty years in preparation for His ministry. Yet, a time came when power was multiplied in Jesus' life, and the speed in which events occurred was significantly accelerated. Representative of this fact is the frequency with which the word *immediately* is used in the Gospels—ten times in the first chapter of Mark alone! It tells us that when the Holy Spirit moves, He does so powerfully and quickly.

We have relied on traditions. We have been hemmed in by human boundaries and limitations that were bred into us from

our culture. Yet something new and wonderful is upon us: The Lord is leading us into
total reliance upon His covenant promises.

We should expect a rapid increase of
answered prayer, heightened divine activity,
and immediate breakthroughs in the days
ahead. Indeed, in many parts of the world,
revival conditions are already explosively
changing the world. We will soon learn that
it is not any harder for God to do something
instantly than for Him to work *gradually*.
We must stop thinking that *gradually* is the
only way God can move.

How can we access this immediate moving
of God in our lives? Perhaps there are many
answers, but one primary condition is in
discovering the power of the New Covenant.
In the truest sense, our spiritual progress is
directly attached to the depth of our revelation of the New Covenant. The more we
understand what Christ has accomplished
for us, the more perfectly we rely upon
Him, and the quicker we will see the hand
of God move.

Yes, we have received forgiveness from
God through the blood, and we have
figuratively applied His blood to the "door-
posts" of our lives. But the shed blood of
Jesus Christ has released much more than
most have attained. In truth, we have
known the first stages of covenant power—

what we are freed from—but we do not know what we are *called to possess.*

The Israelites were delivered out of Egypt that they may possess the Promised Land. So too, through the power of the New Covenant, we have been delivered out of our human sin and limitations into the nature of Christ Himself. We have received God-sized boundaries, heaven-wide assurances, and eternal promises that transcend the weaknesses of our abilities.

As Israel was to follow the priests and the ark of the covenant, so our task is to carefully follow Jesus Christ, our High Priest. He shall guide us into covenant dimensions where the realm of the supernatural becomes not just a distant mystery but rather the abiding place, the "Promised Land" for His New Covenant people!

THE POWER OF THE COVENANT

AS WE STATED PREVIOUSLY, A COVENANT WAS THE highest form of commitment consummated between individuals. The Jewish covenant was made between God and Israel, with Moses serving as mediator. That covenant, however, was conditional, requiring the Israelites fulfill all the demands of the Law. The Old Covenant mediated through Moses was imperfect because Israel continually failed to maintain her relationship to the covenant because of sin.

Just as the Jews are a chosen, covenant people, so Christians are also covenant people. The New Covenant, however, comes to us with far greater promises and unlimited spiritual potential.

First, it is important to understand that the New Covenant was not made directly with us. It was made between the Father and Son for us—two Partners who abide in perfect fulfillment of covenant conditions. Connected to this divine union through spiritual rebirth is the church, serving as the beneficiary of the New Covenant.

The Old Covenant brought great promises; however, it also brought great liabilities. If Israel sinned and did not soon repent, the blessings of the covenant were nullified, and progressively, curses overtook the people. In other words, the covenant was only good if Israel was good. If the Jews violated just one of the commandments, it was as though they were guilty of all. Thus, the burden of fulfillment rested upon Israel, not God. Israel's obedience was the hinge that opened the door to covenant blessings.

The conditions for us in the New Covenant are markedly different. We access the benefits of the New Covenant through faith in God's redemptive work. Our trust is in His works—not ours. This is the glorious wonder of our faith: God covenanted with God on our behalf!

What we receive in the New Covenant is not based on our attainments, but Christ's. The covenant conditions have been eternally settled. We need harbor no fear of rejection by God because of our disobedience. Indeed, the New Covenant between the Father and Son was established precisely for the purpose of pardoning our disobedience!

The terms of the New Covenant were as follows: If Jesus would live His life in holy, sinless purity, never once failing to obey the Father; if He would surrender Himself to the humiliation and suffering of crucifixion and death, God would transfer the penalties, curses, and moral debt owed by mankind to Christ. Everything due sinners would be delivered to Jesus. Divine justice would be served by divine love; mercy would triumph over judgment.

The covenant was enacted not only for all mankind, but for all time as well, eventually reversing the fallen state of creation itself. The cleansing of the universe itself, the creation of the new heavens and earth, and the removal of the curse and its effects all find their origins in the power of the New Covenant.

Those who believe receive the first

installment of redemption. When God looks at His Son's sacrifice, His justice is satisfied. Atonement has been paid: a perfect life in exchange for imperfect lives.

> And when you were dead in your transgressions and the uncircumcision of your flesh, He made you alive together with Him, having forgiven us all our transgressions, having canceled out the certificate of debt consisting of decrees against us and which was hostile to us; and He has taken it out of the way, having nailed it to the cross.
>
> —COLOSSIANS 2:13–14

The New Covenant was fulfilled at the cross. It is there that the certificate of debt consisting of decrees against us, which were hostile to us, was taken out of the way, nailed to the cross of Christ. Your debt has been taken out of the way. The decrees against you have been canceled. Across the face of the "certificate of debt...which was hostile to us" is written, "Paid in full by the blood of the Lamb."

Oh, what a God we serve! The Father sends His only begotten Son—the very essence and substance of Himself—to represent mankind so that God could covenant with God and thus perfectly secure our eternal rescue!

What of the devil? What of the powers of darkness? After proclaiming God's great rescue plan and the divine canceling of debt, Paul addresses the consequence of God's forgiveness of mankind and its effect on the powers of darkness. He reveals that when Christ "disarmed the rulers and authorities [principalities and powers], He made a public display of them, having triumphed over them through Him" (Col. 2:15).

If Satan were a prosecuting attorney and our sins were his charge against us, it is as though they suddenly do not exist. Our iniquities have been "taken out of the way." If there were fines to be paid, Jesus paid them. If punishment due, Jesus took it. Our sins were the weapon in the evil one's hand, which he used effectively to separate us from God. Jesus' sacrifice disarmed this weapon and rendered Satan's accusations against us powerless.

The New Covenant is at the heart of the "truth" that Jesus said will "set you free." Are you free yet? What must you do to receive it? Believe it.

ALL THINGS ARE OURS

YET, NOT ONLY HAVE WE RECEIVED SALVATION,

but Paul asks, "How will He not also with Him freely give us all things?" (Rom. 8:32). In other words, if God would go so far as to *give* His Son, what would He *withhold?* The answer is that He would withhold nothing. The blood covenant has released the heart of God. All the pent-up blessings that Israel could not receive because of sin, God now lavishes upon those who simply enter the New Covenant through receiving Christ.

We must discover—may it be revealed to us even now—how the Father has longed to be gracious to mankind for ages. Indeed, He has secured everything we need pertaining to life and the appropriation of godliness. (See 2 Peter 1:3.)

Everything has been granted us because of the blood covenant. Israel followed the ark of the covenant and entered into the Promised Land. The "land" we are called to inherit is the bounty of God's love! This covenant of full forgiveness is what we are called to follow. This is the security we have going before us in life.

Nothing we have known in our worldly experience compares to the power of the New Covenant. Truly, we have not been this way before.

Paul tells us that God has blessed us "with every spiritual blessing in the heavenly places" (Eph. 1:3). What is this place, "the heavenly places?" It is the spiritual realm, the womb of power and source of influence in this world. "Just as it is written, 'Things which eye has not seen and ear has not heard, and which have not entered the heart of man, all that God has prepared for those who love Him'" (1 Cor. 2:9).

God has prepared blessings for us in the heavenly places. What are these blessings? They represent all we behold in the life of Jesus: the blessing of healing and miracles, of virtue and deliverance. Scripture again tells us, "How will He not also with Him freely give us all things?" (Rom. 8:32).

With Jesus, God "freely" gives us "all things." The operative phrase is "with Jesus." Whatever we see in Jesus defines the range of what God has freely given us. If He would give us His Son, which is His best, how will He not also give whatever provision is needed to meet every human need abundantly?

We have received all because Jesus gave all. Everything we receive is based on what Jesus accomplished in the New Covenant! There is the salvation of loved ones and revival to touch our neighborhoods and cities. Just as the priests carried the covenant ark, and the promises contained in the ark defined Israel's range of victory, so we must redefine the range of our victory based upon the power of the New Covenant. We must allow the blood of Jesus to redefine the boundaries of our reality.

> Now we have received, not the spirit of the world, but the Spirit who is from God, that we might know the things freely given to us by God.
> —1 CORINTHIANS 2:12

Do you know the "things freely given to us by God?" The operative word here is "freely." We do not deserve God's gracious gifts. If we think we can earn them, we cannot receive them. They are ours, not because we have worked for them, but because Jesus died for them. It is not a matter of works, but of faith. Our Christianity is not based on what we do, but upon who Jesus becomes to us.

The gifts of God are free, but they are costly: They come through the blood of the Lamb, received through the power of the New Covenant.

> What then shall we say to these things?
> If God is for us, who is against us?
> —ROMANS 8:31

The nature of Christ and the power of

His kingdom is the land of our inheritance, the land of the covenant God. Whether it is the Jordan ceasing its flow as our feet touch the water or the sick coming forth for healing, all things are ours because of the covenant of God with Christ.

Therefore I say to you, all things for which you pray and ask, believe that you have received them, and they shall be granted you.

—MARK 11:24

8

Believe You
Have Received

It is time to say, "Yes, Lord! I believe!"

WHEN THE LORD heals people and does His great works of grace, and you hear the report of salvations, do not be a cynic and say, "It's too good to be true." A *cynic* is a "habitual doubter." Beware of becoming a cynic, for the promises of God are good, and they are true. Because of the New Covenant, we must stop saying the word "unbelievable" when great miracles and the wonderful gifts of God are discussed. Receive His promise and believe it. It is for you.

We can amass piles of doctrines concerning the New Covenant, but its greatest power is released by divine revelation. Pray for this revelation. Seek God to make this holy truth real. At the cross, God canceled the effects of the curse upon mankind, the prince of the world was judged, Satan was rendered powerless, and the sins of the world were atoned for.

You say, "If He did these things, why is the world in its sorry, present state?" Paul tells us that "we who were the first to hope in Christ should be to the praise of His glory" (Eph. 1:12). Ultimately, all things shall be summed up in Christ, but today the church is the first partaker of the effects of the New Covenant.

It is for us to simply and persistently believe what God has said. Because of Jesus' death, we have been blessed with every spiritual blessing in the heavenly places; we have received all things pertaining to life and godliness; we have been created in the image of Him who created us, in holiness and righteousness. (See Ephesians 4:24.) Notice that all the things the Scriptures say about us are past tense. They have already been given us, and they have been given us, not because we deserved them, but through the greatness of God's love and Jesus' sacrifice.

The more consumed we are with Jesus and what He has done for us, the less we get tangled up in our own unrighteousness. You cannot change yourself by looking at yourself. Listen to what Jesus taught about human nature and its relationship with Himself. He said:

> And as Moses lifted up the serpent in the wilderness, even so must the Son of Man be lifted up; that whoever believes may in Him have eternal life.
> —JOHN 3:14–15

The people of Israel had sinned. They could not cure themselves. They were under the penalty of judgment for their murmuring and rebellion against God. The Lord told Moses to lift up a bronze serpent on a pole. The bronze serpent did not heal anyone until they looked away from themselves and gazed steadfastly upon the bronze serpent.

The pole upon which the bronze serpent was fastened must have been tall to enable all Israel—over three million people—to see it. Perhaps it was carried high throughout the camp. Jesus likened His crucifixion to this event. Christ became sin on our behalf that we might become the righteousness of God. He became like that which destroyed Israel so that He might save Israel. He said that as the serpent was lifted up so must He, that "whoever believes may in Him have eternal life."

The next verse reads:

> For God so loved the world, that He gave His only begotten Son, that whoever believes in Him should not perish, but have eternal life.
> —JOHN 3:16

This is what we are to study, to gaze upon with steadfast attention; this is the truth that brings our healing: God was in Christ reconciling the world unto Himself.

IT IS FINISHED

ALL THESE THINGS HAVE BEEN ACCOMPLISHED FOR us and are part of the eternal covenant between the Father and the Son. It is done. Redemption was accomplished and had nothing to do with our attainment or goodness.

Jesus tells us that accepting His finished work, this New Covenant, is the basis of all true faith. Here is the means through which we access the eternal life, the blessings in the heavenly places. We believe we have already received them through the blood of Jesus.

> Therefore I say to you, all things for which you pray and ask, believe that

you have received them, and they
shall be granted you.

—MARK 11:24

There is no trickery, no mind manipula-
tion here. It is simply a revelation of what
has been accomplished at the cross: fulfillment of a New Covenant between the
Father and Son.

The reason I believe I have received
from God is because of how wonderful
Jesus is and what He has accomplished! It
has nothing to do with my personal goodness, and everything to do with Him. Let
me state it again: Our salvation is not based
on what we do, but upon who Jesus
becomes to us. To fully abandon ourselves
into the power of the New Covenant is to
discover the kingdom of God.

In the next section, we shall discuss
defeating witchcraft and its power. Yet,
before we can conquer our enemies, we
must know the power of Jesus' blood. Let
us pray fervently for a deepening of revelation concerning the covenant.

Let us pray:

*O God, topple the limitations of our
minds! Destroy that thinking in us
that still relies upon our own righteousness when we come to You. Help*

*us to fully trust in the blood of Christ
and the power released by You through
the New Covenant. In Jesus' name. Amen.*

Now the God of peace, who brought
up from the dead the great Shepherd
of the sheep through the blood of the
eternal covenant, even Jesus our
Lord, equip you in every good thing
to do His will, working in us that
which is pleasing in His sight,
through Jesus Christ, to whom be the
glory forever and ever. Amen.

—HEBREWS 13:20–21

When He had taken a cup and given
thanks, He said, "Take this and share
it among yourselves; for I say to you,
I will not drink of the fruit of the vine
from now on until the kingdom of
God comes." And when He had
taken some bread and given thanks,
He broke it and gave it to them
saying, "This is my body which is
given for you; do this in remem-
brance of Me." And in the same way
He took the cup after they had eaten,
saying, "This cup which is poured
out for you is the new covenant in
My blood."

—LUKE 22:17–20

Part Two:
Exposing Witchcraft

The eternal God is a dwelling place,
And underneath are the everlasting arms;
And He drove out the enemy
from before you,
And said, "Destroy!"
So Israel dwells in security,
The fountain of Jacob secluded,
In a land of grain and new wine;
His heavens also drop down dew.
Blessed are you, O Israel;
Who is like you, a people saved by the LORD,
Who is the shield of your help,
And the sword of your majesty!
So your enemies shall cringe before you,
And you shall tread upon their high places.

—DEUTERONOMY 33:27–29

9

Keys Unlock Gates

Heaven has keys that can unlock hell.

A s we enter part two of this book, it is
important that we recall Christ's word
to His followers:

> I will build My church; and the gates
> of Hades shall not overpower it. I will
> give you the keys of the kingdom of
> heaven; and whatever you shall bind
> on earth shall be bound in heaven,
> and whatever you shall loose on
> earth shall be loosed in heaven.
> —Matthew 16:18–19

When we read these words of Christ's,

many of us picture a determined, aggressive church charging boldly toward the gates of hell. Such images of spiritual warfare are typical today and certainly a vast improvement over the passive, selfish attitudes that infiltrated the church in previous years.

Yet, there is more in this text than the bold confrontation of the strongholds of hell. Between the lines, there is the mention of strategies: the "keys" of the kingdom of God.

Let us isolate two words in Jesus' teaching that will broaden our understanding of spiritual warfare. Those two words are "keys" and "gates." Simply put, keys unlock gates. Reversing the sequence of the Lord's thoughts, Jesus promised to grant us the keys of the kingdom of heaven . . . and the gates of hell will not prevail against us. Note that He did not say He was giving us keys to the kingdom, but the keys of heaven. The goal is not to unlock heaven, for Jesus has already done that. Jesus is saying that heaven has keys that can unlock hell.

SETTING THE CAPTIVES FREE

WHEN JESUS CAME, HE PLAINLY DEMONSTRATED that He had spiritual keys that unlocked hell's gates. In fact, in His first public teaching He declared that this confrontation with hell was His main mission. He said:

> The Spirit of the Lord is upon Me,
> because He anointed Me to preach
> the gospel to the poor. He has sent
> Me to proclaim release to the cap-
> tives, and recovery of sight to the
> blind, to set free those who are
> downtrodden, to proclaim the favor-
> able year of the Lord.
> —LUKE 4:18–19

The Father specifically anointed Jesus to go to four main people groups: the economically and morally "poor"; those who had spiritually become "captives" of demons; those who were "blind" but desired vision; and those who were emotionally wounded—the "downtrodden." The goal of Christ's ministry was to find these people and set them free.

Before we dash off "binding and loosing" every evil thing we can imagine, we should also remember that Jesus said of Himself, "I have the keys of death and of Hades" (Rev. 1:18).

If we will be successful in spiritual warfare, we must go beyond trying to apply spiritual principles against the devil; we need the anointing of Jesus to set captives free, which only comes from the heart of Jesus.

In every spiritual confrontation, in each strategic assault against the strongholds of hell over our soul, churches, and cities, we must first recognize that Jesus alone is God's antidote for all our world's ills. As we dwell in the shelter of Christ's presence, Jesus has the particular keys that can unlock the gates of hell and release captives.

In this regard we shall discuss the phenomenon of witchcraft in our society. We will look at how witchcraft functions and our authority in Christ to combat it. However, the most important key we can find is Christ's compassion, for a number of those who are involved in the occult were once disillusioned children in Christian homes. Others are yet children who, in dabbling in the occult, became ensnared; still others have been lifelong victims of satanic abuse. Jesus wants these people back.

Oh that My people would listen to Me,
That Israel would walk in My ways!
I would quickly subdue their enemies,
And turn My hand against
their adversaries.

—PSALM 81:13–14

10

Exposing Witchcraft

Fighting against the occult
is an increasing battle.

Over the past years, our society has taken an increasingly more tolerant view of witchcraft and the occult in America. Indeed, under the guise of the New Age movement, the practice of witchcraft has been mainstreamed into our nation. Consequently, we are seeing schools and, in some cases, even churches corrupted with occult beliefs.

One sign of the times is seen in Salem, Massachusetts, home of the historic Salem witchcraft trials. In a community that once executed four people for allegedly practicing witchcraft, today four thousand practitioners of "the craft" live and enjoy freedom in the Salem area. Witchcraft has become a locally supported cottage industry.

While Salem is an extreme case, the fact is that our nation as a whole has opened itself to the practice of witchcraft. Law enforcement agencies throughout the country are reluctant to prosecute those practicing witchcraft. This is in spite of the fact that many satanists habitually use drugs and are engaged in violent criminal activities. On occasion, police departments have been infiltrated by members of the occult, further hindering the processes of justice.

While we are not advocating a return to the death penalty for witchcraft, we must find a truly Christian response to this demonic intrusion. We can no longer remain ignorant of the enemy's tactics. The assault of witchcraft must be discerned and a Christ-inspired strategy initiated.

Many whom Jesus Christ is calling to Himself are trapped in witchcraft. We must know His heart for these people. How can we find the Lord's wisdom in order that those practicing witchcraft can be delivered, their curses broken, and the people they have targeted released?

A BRIEF OVERVIEW: WITCHCRAFT'S HISTORY

REGARDLESS OF THE NATION IN WHICH IT emerges, witchcraft manifests similarly throughout the world. The differences lie in the degree to which it takes over a community. The fact is, in many simple cultures, witches (also called witch doctors, medicine men, or shamans) enjoy unchallenged places of influence.

What we identify in North America as witchcraft can for the most part be traced back to pre-Christian fertility cults that existed in pagan Europe. Witchcraft also came to this continent from Africa and Asia. Throughout medieval times, the European root of these demonic religions actually coexisted alongside Christianity, although in ever-diminishing roles.

Witches derived their power from evil spirits, which were revered or at least feared by the community. Persons who were thought to have access to the spirit world were also revered or feared. Witch doctors were expected to cure the sick, make rain, and assure success in the hunt and in war. In a culture where witchcraft ruled, the witch (or witch doctor) was judge, jury, and executioner in societal affairs; he was second only to the tribal chief.

As the church entered the beginning of the Dark Ages, she grew relatively lenient toward witchcraft. Persons who were proven to have practiced witchcraft were required only to do penance. Clergymen, struggling to consolidate the power of the church in Europe, recognized that all-out conflict with the remaining devotees of the old religion might be disastrous. Not only did they frequently tolerate the local paganism, but they often participated in its witchcraft.

Jesus warned that in time the "wheat and tares" would grow side by side. We do not have to go far to see the influence ancient paganism had on a number of Christian traditions. Consider that "Easter" was originally "Eastre," the name of a pagan goddess of fertility who was worshiped during the spring in Old England. The first-century disciples honored Christ's Resurrection during the Feast of Passover. The "eggs and bunnies," which we have identified with Easter, were originally pagan symbols of sexual fertility!

Consider also Christmas. This winter holiday originally marked the Roman festival, Saturnalia, which commemorated the winter solstice. According to the new Webster's dictionary, it was a time of orgies and excessive revelry. *Funk & Wagnall's Encyclopedia* tells us it was also a time of gift giving and general goodwill. Today, we honor Jesus' birthday during this time. But for those who do not know Christ, it is still a time of revelry.

CHRISTIAN OPPOSITION

As THE CHURCH GREW IN NUMBERS AND SOCIAL influence, it took a more open resistance to witchcraft, becoming more vocal against the disintegrating paganism. Those who remained active in witchcraft reacted as we would expect; at various times during the next thousand years, many witches were emboldened to commit great horrors.

There was a time in thirteenth-century Germany when a witch's greatest prize was to kidnap and offer to Satan a Christian's unbaptized child. To counteract this atrocity, German Christians began baptizing their babies just after birth. The practice ended the kidnappings, but it propagated a new doctrine, which, in a short time, became a cornerstone of Christian orthodoxy in Germany: infant baptism!

This opposition of the church to witch-craft heightened during the seventeenth century, culminating in the infamous In-quisition, which was fueled by witch hunts. More than one hundred thousand persons were burned alive, drowned, or hanged in

Germany alone. The terrible tragedy was that the vast majority of those who died were not witches, but Anabaptists, whose worst crime was refusing the doctrine of infant baptism!

WHAT WE LEARN FROM THIS

TO OVERREACT TO WITCHCRAFT IS, PERHAPS, WORSE than completely ignoring it. God does not want us to be ignorant of, nor overly focused upon, Satan's devices. Until Jesus returns, we will have various forms and expressions of witchcraft in our society. No doubt they will become more blatant as wickedness descends from shades of gray to utter blackness. The Lord does not want us to direct our attention toward occult activity beyond recognizing it as a demonic phenomenon, discerning it, and eliminating our vulnerability to it.

How shall I curse,
whom God has not cursed?
And how can I denounce,
*whom the L*ORD
has not denounced?

—NUMBERS 23:8

11

How Witchcraft Works

*It is our heart's attitude that draws
to us God's blessing or His curse.*

I T IS SIGNIFICANT that just before Israel entered Canaan, Balak, the Midianite king,
sought to use witchcraft to stop Israel. However, every time the sorcerer Balaam opened
his mouth to curse Israel, blessings poured
forth instead. Balaam asserted, "How shall I
curse, whom God has not cursed? And how
can I denounce, whom the LORD has not
denounced?" (Num. 23:8). If we study this
text, we can find a basic understanding of
witchcraft and how the transfer of curses
occurs.

In the truest sense, there is no power in
the universe except that which comes from

God. God is the sole Creator; He is the prime mover of all creation. John tells us that all things came into being through Him and apart from Him nothing exists. Hebrews tells us that, even now, the Lord is "upholding and maintaining and guiding and propelling the universe by His mighty word of power" (Heb. 1:3, AMP).

God's "mighty . . . power" is revealed in the universe through spontaneous and biological creation and through the natural laws of physics. It is also unveiled through spiritual and moral laws, which govern our relationships.

Every moment of every day, in every aspect of our lives, we are governed by the interconnected, congruous expressions of God's power. As independent as we think we are, every breath, each thought, and every movement we make has its existence in the continuum of God's energy. There is nothing and no one hidden from His sight, for in Him we move and exist and have our being (Acts 17:28).

Yet, we are not robots. There is a place in the expanse of God's omniscience where, to facilitate His plan to make man in His image, He allows us freedom of choice. If we obey Him, our lives move forward along the stream of His blessing. Here, He orchestrates all things to work for our good. Or, if we turn away from Him, we eventually position ourselves under the weight of His judgment. As such, we leave ourselves indefensible against evil. The Bible describes our freedom as the choice between God's blessing or His curse, and every soul has this choice. If we walk in obedience, we actually become a blessing. However, if we rebel against Him, our existence is under His wrath and our lives are accursed. An individual might be rich and famous but inwardly accursed and wretched, or one could be materially poor but inwardly blessed and full of life's truest joys. God's blessings are manifested in the quality of our lives, not the quality of our possessions.

"The curse of the LORD is on the house of the wicked, but He blesses the dwelling of the righteous" (Prov. 3:33). Perhaps it is difficult for us to imagine our loving Father cursing anything. Yet, God's curse upon evil is motivated by His love, for He uses His judgment to prod the wicked toward righteousness and peace.

God's "wrath," His "judgment" or "sentence against sin," and His "curse" are all interchangeable terms. His wrath abides on "all ungodliness and unrighteousness" (Rom. 1:18). Before we were saved, we "walked . . . according to the prince of the power of the air, of the spirit that is now working in the sons of disobedience . . . by nature [we were] children of wrath, even as the rest" (Eph. 2:2–3).

God's wrath can be as broad and obvious as the earth deluged by the Great Flood, or it can be as elementary as the consequences of our own selfishness. It is our heart's attitude that draws to us God's blessing or His curse. If we love His blessing, we become a blessing to others. If we harden our hearts in rebellion, we inherit His wrath. As it is written:

> He also loved cursing, so it came to him; and he did not delight in blessing, so it was far from him. But he clothed himself with cursing as with his garment, and it entered into his body like water, and like oil into his bones.
>
> —PSALM 109:17–18

SATAN: MASTER MANIPULATOR

IN ORDER TO APPLY THE POWER OF COVENANT prayer to the effects of witchcraft, it is important to know how witchcraft functions. The devil has no power to originate anything; he can only manipulate what already is under the judgment or wrath of God. All sin is under God's curse, and whatever is under God's curse is accessible to evil spirits.

Christians are not exempt from this. If we sow to the flesh, we will reap corruption. Paul says, "For he who does wrong will receive the consequences of the wrong which he has done, and that without partiality" (Col. 3:25). Jesus told a parable about a man who refused to show mercy to others after receiving mercy himself. The consequence? His lord was "moved with anger" and "handed him over to the torturers until he should repay all that was owed him." Then Jesus said, "So shall My heavenly Father also do to you, if each of you does not forgive his brother from your heart" (Matt. 18:34–35).

The Lord does not have to personally "hand" someone over to "torturers." Sin carries its own punishment. Even sin in a Christian's heart will eventually reap corruption and make us vulnerable to evil spirits if we fail to repent and walk humbly with our God.

God's greatest blessing abides upon the nature of Christ. Wherever we are walking as Jesus walked, in love and purity of heart, we are enriched and protected by God's blessing. Even the desire to walk like Christ draws the Father's blessing, for such a soul is quick to repent; its humility draws grace from God.

HEAVEN'S FENCE

BALAAM'S STATEMENT, "HOW SHALL I CURSE, whom God has not cursed? And how can I denounce, whom the Lord has not denounced?" (Num. 23:8), shows us that God has put a fence around the devil. Only those areas of man's heart that are already under divine judgment because of persistent sin are openly vulnerable to curses and the effects of witchcraft.

Having said that, let me now qualify it. There are occasions when the Lord, for His purpose, grants Satan permission to sift a servant of God, as with Job and Peter (Job 1:12; Luke 22:31–32). In each case, however, the devil had to appeal to God before the spiritual attack was made. The outcome of this attack would serve God's higher purposes. It would build character and humility in His servant. So, unless otherwise allowed by God, satanic activity is limited to what is already under the judgment of God.

We see this portrayed in Moses' confrontation with Pharaoh. Moses brought God's decree of judgment—His curse on the Egyptians and their "gods." Yet, the Egyptian diviners were able to duplicate a number of God's judgments, including turning the Nile to blood and sending the plague of frogs. (See Exodus 7:22; 8:7.) How could Pharaoh's sorcerers reproduce the plagues of Moses? They could only duplicate what was already under the judgment of God. Notice also: Although they could duplicate God's judgments, they could not stop them.

This is the basis of how most witchcraft and occult power works: Satan is limited to what is under God's judgment. The devil cannot revoke what God has cursed, and he cannot harm what God has blessed. Proverbs 26:2 tells us, "Like a sparrow in its flitting, like a swallow in its flying, so a curse without cause does not alight."

God will not allow a curse to land without cause. Sin is the landing strip in a person's soul upon which a curse alights. Just as "death" entered the world "through sin" (Rom. 5:12), so death cannot enter where there is no sin.

Thus, the key to walking free from the effects of witchcraft is to walk in obedience to God and under the shelter of His blessing. It is here that we find God's antidote for evil. For Satan cannot curse what God has blessed.

For He delivered us from the domain of darkness, and transferred us to the kingdom of His beloved Son, in whom we have redemption, the forgiveness of sins.

—COLOSSIANS 1:13–14

12

God's Great Mercy

*No sorcery can stand against
Christlikeness.*

THE LORD'S WILL for ancient Israel was to
follow God and obey His laws. By the
time the nation of Israel was about to leave
the wilderness, they had attained this level of
obedience. Consequently, they were walking
in the blessing of God. When Balaam, the
premier sorcerer in the Middle East, tried to
curse Israel, he was unable to do so. Each
time he opened his mouth, only blessings
came forth. Balaam proclaimed, "There is
no sorcery against Jacob, nor any divination against Israel" (Num. 23:23, NKJV).

Why? Because God "has blessed, and I
cannot reverse it. He has not observed

iniquity in Jacob" (vv. 20–21, NKJV).

There was no witchcraft against Israel because Israel was not under God's judgment for sin; it was under His blessing for righteousness. For a Christian, the definition of sin is not merely being in violation of the Mosaic law but refusing to submit to Christlikeness. God's will is not just that we keep the commandments, but that we become like Jesus.

This text concerning ancient Israel is especially relevant for us today, for as Israel was about to engage in its greatest, most successful warfare, so the church finds herself on the threshold of a similar day. What did Satan raise up as a last and final deterrent against Israel? Witchcraft. And what do we see rising ever more blatantly in our land? Witchcraft!

THE GIFT

WE HAVE LEARNED THAT A CURSE, WITH ITS associated demonic activity and cargo of death, can be "cast upon" or "bound" to a person in rebellion against God. And, we have discovered that one aspect of God's judgment upon sin is increased vulnerability to demonic assault and witchcraft.

So also, God's blessing, with its angelic protection and cargo of life, can be committed to us as well. In the purest sense, Christ alone is the divine antidote against curses and the assault of witchcraft. The combination of Jesus' work on the cross and His nature in our hearts provides a perfect haven for all who flee to Him. In Him, there is no darkness at all; if we are in Him, we are therefore sheltered from the effects of God's judgment against sin as well as from Satan's exploitation of what God has cursed.

Apart from Christ, humanity exists unprotected against witchcraft. However, Christ is not only God's plan of refuge against witchcraft, He is a refuge against the entire realm of sin and death. The fact is, all mankind has sinned and fallen short of the glory of God. God's judgment upon mankind is not to condemn us, but to compel us to run to Christ, who alone is our shelter in this world.

In an eternal sense, from the first moment we come to Christ, all our sins are "legally" paid for with Christ's blood, and all curses are broken at Christ's cross. Spiritually speaking, we were delivered from the domain of darkness and transferred into the kingdom of His Son (Col. 1:13).

This deliverance is true wealth laid up for us in heaven's bank. However, if we do not draw upon it and use it, we will remain poor and spiritually impoverished.

Thus, a twofold experience occurred when we were born again: We received every spiritual blessing in the heavenly places in Christ, and we embarked on a journey of faith and obedience to appropriate them.

Though our spirits are now alive to God, our souls are still imperfect. If we willfully harbor rebellion toward God, we still leave ourselves exposed to witchcraft and the effects of curses. To stir us to pursue godliness, therefore, the Lord reduces His protection on the areas of sin within us.

It is also true that we ourselves may not have sinned, but we might be living under the curse of ancestral sins. These are the sins that have been passed down to us from our parents. To break ancestral curses, we must identify the un-Christlike behavior we have inherited from our forefathers and then renounce it. Submitting our hearts to Christ for cleansing and ongoing transformation, we determine to build our lives upon the nature of Christ.

A curse cannot penetrate what God has blessed. What is it that God has blessed? God has blessed the church with every spiritual blessing in the heavenly places in Christ (Eph. 1:3). All our blessings are "in Christ." Our substitute for the penalty of sin is Christ crucified; our buffer against death and curses is Christ resurrected and abiding within us.

THE LORD'S STRATEGY

CONFRONTATION WITH OCCULT POWERS SHALL increase in the days ahead. It is a fact that today part of the daily ritual of satanists is to release curses on pastors, their families, and churches. If the life purpose of that minister is less than the transformation of his soul, the effects of witchcraft can torment his mind, destroy his marriage, and/or divide his church.

Remember, God's will requires us to become Christlike. To facilitate His purpose, God allows whatever is not Christlike within us to remain vulnerable to spiritual assault. In the following chapter, we deal with overcoming curses. We emphasize the need to become like Christ, and Jesus tells us to "bless those who curse you" (Luke 6:28).

While we take authority over the spirit of witchcraft and renounce the effects of its curse, we must also become aggressive in our love. We are not warring against individuals but against the spirits that enslave them. We cannot overcome evil with evil; we must overcome evil with love.

Therefore be imitators of God, as beloved children; and walk in love.

—EPHESIANS 5:1–2

13

Symptoms of Witchcraft

The Lord accommodates evil to bring forth godly character in us.

To DEAL WITH witchcraft, we must understand its effects. As Christians, we must become a people who exercise the gift of discernment.

Let us examine some of the characteristic symptoms that can be observed when witchcraft hits a Christian or a church.

1. When a Christian is under an assault of witchcraft, he becomes increasingly disoriented or confused; he might even become clumsy. Satan wants to cloud your vision, thus stopping you

from reaching your destiny in God. The individual under attack cannot connect with his spiritual vision; his motivation is either gone or lacking.

2. When one is targeted by curses, he will feel emotionally drained or debilitated. Those who have been the object of spiritual curses will carry a darkness, a cloud, in their countenance. The back of their neck is tight; a band of oppression around their head manifests as a headache. The person might assume he is sick, but it is not the flu. It is witchcraft.

3. Often the curses released from witchcraft will arouse a number of inordinate fears that plague the mind. The theater of the individual's imagination will be targeted: At center stage, grotesque images will flash across the mind. The individual will be further drained by lack of deep or restful sleep.

4. When curses are aimed at a congregation, interchurch relationships will experience constant problems, distracting the body of Christ from its primary focus and calling.

Irritation levels will be high; patience will be low. People will be more likely to complain about one another. Gossip and backbiting will increase proportionately. Rebellion against church leaders will seem justified and the temptation to withdraw from fellowship will be strong.

It is vital to note that any or all of these symptoms may be evident, and the cause may not be witchcraft. However, once we ascertain that we are truly fighting a spiritual enemy, victory is near.

PUTTING ON CHRIST

TO WIN THIS BATTLE, WE MUST UNDERSTAND WHY the Lord allows evil in the first place. From the beginning, God's plan has been to create mankind in His image, according to His likeness. To facilitate His eternal purpose, the Lord accommodates evil to bring forth godly character in us.

In other words, we would never ascend to the heights of Christlike love, which loves even one's adversary, without there being actual enemies to perfect our love.

God cannot establish within us a pure heart and a steadfast spirit without allowing genuine temptations and obstacles that must be refused and overcome. The reason the Lord even tolerates evil in the world is to produce a righteousness within us that not only withstands the assault of evil, but it grows stronger and brighter in the midst of it.

Therefore, to deal with witchcraft, we must understand that the Lord's primary objective is not the removal of wickedness from society, but the transformation of our hearts to Christlikeness. As we become like Jesus—that is, loving our enemies, blessing those who curse us—Christ Himself literally and tangibly manifests Himself in our spirits. It is the transformed soul that dwells in the stronghold of God.

Enter His gates with thanksgiving,
And His courts with praise.

—Psalm 100:4

14

God's Shelter
Against Witchcraft

*God's promise is not to keep us from
conflict, but to be with us in conflict.*

L ET'S LOOK AGAIN at the symptoms that
accompany the assault of witchcraft and
apply the principle of transformation.

1. *How do we break the effect of
   curses and confusion that block
   our vision?*

We bless those who curse us. Even if we
do not know specifically who is directing a
curse toward us, we pray a blessing on
them. In other words, we ask God to bless
them with the same blessing we have experienced in our repentance and coming to

Christ. We bless and curse not.

This is vital. Too many Christians become bitter and angry in the conflict. If we descend into hatefulness, we have already lost the battle against witchcraft. We must cooperate with God in turning what was meant for evil into a greater good within us. This is why we bless those who would curse us. It is not only for their sakes, but to preserve our own soul from its natural response toward hatred.

While silent prayer is certainly an acceptable form of communication with God, it is our experience that audible prayer is both more forceful and effective with regard to spiritual warfare. A typical example of a prayer against witchcraft and curses would be the following:

> *Heavenly Father, You know the battle that is coming against me/us. I pray that You would forgive those who are serving the devil. Lord, I know You said that those who bless us, You would bless, and those who curse us, You would curse. Yet, Father, these people are already under Your curse. Therefore, I pray that You would pour out Your redemptive blessings—those very blessings that shatter darkness with light, that overcome evil with*

*good, that bring hope to the hopeless
and life to the dead. And I ask these
things, Heavenly Father, so that You
might fulfill the redemptive purposes
You revealed in Your Son, Jesus Christ
and satisfy the longing of Your heart.
Amen.*

2. *How do we throw off the power of
   debilitation and oppression?*

We put on the mantle of praise for the
spirit of heaviness. The church is, by biblical definition, the house of the Lord, the
temple of God. The purpose of the temple
was not to "house" God, for even the
heaven of heavens cannot contain Him.
The temple was created to offer worship to
the Almighty and to provide a place of
access for us in God's habitation.

Thus, the Holy Spirit unites us so that we
can provide a living temple where we offer
continual worship to God. The battle against
us seeks to keep us from that purpose.

If you are under an assault of witchcraft,
begin to listen to praise tapes in your home
or car. Sing along with them, letting your
heart reach to the Lord. Build a buffer of
worship around your soul. Become
thankful for all that God has given you. The
Scripture says we "enter His gates with

thanksgiving, and His courts with praise" (Ps. 100:4). Then we can pray this prayer for deliverance from oppression.

> *Heavenly Father, You have sought for worshipers, those who will worship You in spirit and in truth. In the midst of this battle, I choose to be Your worshiper. I enter Your gates with thanksgiving. Thank You, Lord Jesus, for saving me, for delivering me from evil, and for the many times You answered my prayers and provided for me. Thank You for all the spiritual blessings You have won for me!*
>
> *Now, in the name of Jesus, I break the power of oppression. I pray for those in my church, as well as Christians throughout my city, to be free also from this oppression. Lord, bring forth a worshiping army, a warring priesthood that shall glorify You in the earth! Amen.*

3. How do we overcome fear?

The Scripture tells us that perfect love casts out fear (1 John 4:18). God has not given us a spirit of fear, but of power, love, and a sound or disciplined mind (2 Tim. 1:7). Satan is a liar and the father of lies.

The devil cannot tell the truth. No matter what Satan tells you, it is not the truth but a perversion of truth.

Jesus also said that Satan is a murderer. Whenever we believe the devil instead of God, the quality of our life proportionally declines; something in us dies, and it dies because we believed a lie. Therefore, we must stop listening to Satan and simply do what the Lord tells us to do.

You ask, "But what if I get hurt?" Being a Christian is not a guarantee that we will not be hurt. Peter tells us, "Therefore, since Christ has suffered in the flesh, arm yourselves also with the same purpose" (1 Pet. 4:1). It is one thing to know that Jesus Christ died for the sins of the world; it is quite another to hear Him tell us, "Come, follow Me" (Luke 18:22). The fears that bind us are often the result of the wavering, unresolved condition of our will. Once we decide to truly follow Christ, the bondage of fear can be overcome.

Where then, you ask, is the divine weapon or the stronghold of God? The Lord never promised us immunity from pain. There will be times when we hurt. Yet, through the love of Christ, our inner person will not be injured. Jesus said we would be "delivered up even by parents and brothers and relatives and friends, and they will put some of you to death, and you will be hated by all on account of My name. Yet not a hair of your head will perish" (Luke 21:16–18).

God's promise is not to keep us *from* conflict, but to be with us *in* conflict. Though we are put to death, every part of our lives shall experience resurrection: "Not a hair . . . will perish."

Indeed, part of our weaponry against the threats of Satan is our knowledge that death cannot hold us. The devil cannot torment us with the fear of dying if we know that death is but a meeting with God, and our departure from earth is but an arrival in heaven.

Let us once again pray:

> *Lord God, forgive me for my fears. I confess that I have been seeking to save my life when You, in fact, have called me to lose it for Your sake. By the power of Your Spirit, I renounce fear. God has not given me a spirit of fear! Father, I submit to the vision and courage of Your Son, Jesus, that I might live in accordance with Your will no matter what the cost.*
>
> *I also pray for others in the body of Christ who might be struggling against inordinate fears and frightening*

imaginations. In the name of Jesus, I bind the spirit of fear, and I pray that, according to Your promise, You will deliver Your people from all their fears. In Jesus' name. Amen.

4. *To end the assault against the congregation—the constant irritations, division, and strife among brethren—we must expose the work of the devil.*

Thousands of churches have gained the upper hand in their battle against darkness by simply recognizing that people are not our real enemy—the devil is. Fathers, mothers, pastors, intercessors, and Christian workers of all kinds must possess this basic knowledge of spiritual warfare and the willingness to exercise authority.

When the enemy seeks to bring us to a place of contention or division with one or more people, we must discern this satanic activity as a plot to keep us all from a blessing that God intended for us. Thus, we must turn quickly to intercession for that person or church.

This prayer posture must expand beyond our immediate church relationships into the citywide body of Christ. We are our brother's keeper. We must recognize that if we are to be effective in resisting the enemy, the church will have to become a house of prayer.

> *Lord, we ask You to grant us the gift of discernment. Forgive us for judging one another and for failing to see the work of the enemy who seeks to divide us. Father, we submit to the mind of Christ; we ask for His perception so that we would have insight into what You are doing in the church.*
>
> *Lord, we also ask for boldness to defend one another from the voice of accusation and suspicion. Help us, Lord, to pray when we hear a rumor, to stand in the gap when we see a fault, and to become a house of covenant prayer for the church in this city. In Jesus' name. Amen.*

Let him who means to love life and see good days refrain his tongue from evil and his lips from speaking guile.

—1 PETER 3:10

15

"Witchcraft" in the Church

*Seeking God for discernment
must be our first priority.*

W E HAVE DEALT with witchcraft as it comes against us from outside the body of Christ. However, there is another means through which Satan binds congregations with curses. It is also witchcraft, but the people whom the devil uses are not satanists—they are misled Christians. Gossip and backbiting among Christians are primary gates through which curses and witchcraft gain access into the church.

Until the body of Christ learns to pray for one another, we will continually find ourselves being manipulated by demons who exploit the prayerlessness of Christians.

Consider this: The most common activity of Christians when they discover sin or failure in the church is not to weep and pray but to descend into the darkness of gossip. Such unbridled talk brings what amounts to a curse against the individual who has stumbled.

Let us assume a brother in Christ, we will call him "Bob," has spent a weekend drinking. He has been a Christian for ten years but was an alcoholic prior to his conversion. This is the third time in the past ten years that he has stumbled. Three people who know his situation are sitting in a room at church, talking about him. The conversation sounds like this:

"Did you hear what Bob did?" said the first person. "He was out drinking from Friday afternoon until Sunday morning."

"Well, that's not the only time he's done that," replies the second person. "How can he call himself a Christian?"

"It makes me furious," says the third. "The money he spent was food money for his family. I've always wondered about him; I never could believe that he was really a Christian!"

And on they talk until, quite unannounced, the door opens and in walks Bob himself! The conversation plunges to a murmur and tapers off into an artificial greeting: "It's nice to see you."

But it is not "nice." And, after that first glance, no one even sees Bob, for the gaze of everyone in the group has dropped to the floor. Each person searches desperately for nothing in particular.

What Bob stepped into was not *talk*—it was *witchcraft*. Of course, it was not pre-Christian European or African witchcraft, but it did basically the same thing to Bob: It ministered death to him. He felt it, and they felt it. *Death*. It manifested all over the room; like a shroud, it covered everybody.

But, let's imagine there was another room at the church, and in it three other people were meeting. These three also knew Bob, but they are part of the intercession team. Their meeting is not to discuss Bob's situation but to pray for him. At various times they cry when they pray.

"O God, You know how Bob's dad was an alcoholic and how You delivered Bob from that bondage ten years ago," the first intercessor prays. "Lord, for Your name's sake, don't let him return to the bondage of alcoholism!"

"Lord, You have kept Bob sober for the past three years!" the next one prays. "For over a thousand days, he has walked clean in this area. Lord, return to him in Your mercy. Raise him up again."

The third intercessor speaks, "Lord, help us to help him. Lord, right now we pray against the accuser of the brethren that wants to condemn Bob and wipe him right out of the kingdom. Lord, we rebuke that spirit in Jesus' name!"

And on they continue until, to their great joy, Bob wanders into the room where they are kneeling. In an instant, the three spring to their feet and hug Bob, letting him know of their love and faith for him, encouraging him to get back on the path with Christ.

Can you see the difference between the two groups? The first is ministering *death;* the second is pouring out *life*. The first group is actually practicing a form of witchcraft under the influence of a religious spirit; the second group is bringing the intercession of Christ before God, and a brother is being saved.

PUT LIFE IN THOSE WORDS!

THIS PRACTICE BY CHRISTIANS OF MINISTERING death instead of life is not limited to immediate church relationships. A congregation can be under a spirit of witchcraft in their attitude about their pastor. The Scriptures tell us, "Rebellion is as the sin of divination" (1 Sam. 15:23).

If you have a problem with the pastor,

pray for him. If you feel that the Lord is calling you to go to another church, you do not have to rebel against your present church in order to leave it. Ask your current pastor to bless you. If there is some conflict, make sure you both forgive each other and are committed to praying for each other. Ask him to call the church where you are going and communicate to your new pastor any insight or support he might have. When it is time to finally move on, make sure that you give your blessing to the ministry and people you leave.

At River of Life Church where I am the senior minister, it is our policy to bless the individuals who want to go to another church, thanking God for our time together. If they are willing, we will bring them before our congregation and "gift wrap" them with our love, admonishing them to consider themselves a blessing from us to their next place of fellowship.

Whatever you do, do not go in rebellion. If you do, you will open the door for witchcraft. Once you become judgmental, you also put yourself under God's judgment. Stay submissive to God, and keep your spirit right. You and all those involved with your transition will benefit from God's blessing rather than obtaining His judgment, which accompanies a rebellious attitude.

Another area where witchcraft can emerge is in the ministry itself. As pastors and counselors, it is easy to slip into gossiping about people in your congregation. To talk negatively about church members seriously jeopardizes their growth potential in your church.

The practice of pastors, elders, or deacons talking about a church member in a derogatory manner—a manner without prayer and love—also opens the door for curses to enter that congregation. Wherever there is slander without supplication and gossip without going to God, the spirit of witchcraft is being ministered through your words. You are actually being used by Satan to make your church situation worse!

Let us expand this into the context of our citywide, inter-church relationships. Again, if we are not praying for each other, the spirit of witchcraft and death can actually infiltrate and divide us. If you have a problem with a church in your community, go to God about the matter. Find His heart before you talk to people. If you go first to Christ, you will find that He is more concerned for their welfare than you imagined.

You ask, "What if a real heresy or a legitimate need is occurring in a church?" Before we begin our own inquisition, we should seek the Lord for His view as well as the priority He places on correcting what we perceive as wrong. Perhaps there are other problems or personal issues that, by speaking the Lord's word of encouragement to the immediate need, the entire church might later be open to hear our other concerns.

Seeking God for discernment must be our first priority. How do we do that? Proverbs gives us a wonderful model. Solomon wrote:

> Make your ear attentive to wisdom, incline your heart to understanding; for if you cry for discernment, lift your voice for understanding; if you seek her as silver, and search for her as for hidden treasures; then you will discern the fear of the LORD, and discover the knowledge of God.
> —PROVERBS 2:2–5

There is a difference between having *knowledge about God* and gaining *God's own knowledge* concerning a situation. We need the Lord's perspective about every matter. Have we not often made a situation worse by approaching it without truly knowing the Lord's heart? When we see as He sees, we are positioned in a more understanding view than our own. Although we may have problems with the people in a particular church, we must remember that

Christ died for them. Certainly, He loves them as much as He loves us.

Therefore, before we leave a particular church because of some apparent need, we must pray for that congregation, earnestly seeking God to gain His knowledge of the situation. A month is not too long to lift your voice for understanding and to search for the hidden treasures of the Lord's discernment. Once you gain God's heart, He may guide you to remain in that church, seeing it with Christ's heart and from His perspective. The key is finding the mind of Christ and proceeding in His redemptive attitude.

THE WORST PLACE FOR WITCHCRAFT

PERHAPS THE WORST PLACE FOR GOSSIP AND FAULT-finding to occur is in the home. Often the prevailing spiritual atmosphere is not one of peace but is actual witchcraft coming against a child through an angry or embittered parent.

When God gave you children, He also provided love so you could pray effectively for them. Let your love express itself before God in intercessory prayer. Never spend more time complaining about your child than you do praying for him or her. If you have to keep praying for years, then do it. If the spiritual atmosphere in your home is one of "death," you are simply destroying your own life.

There are times when a curse comes upon a family through a child, usually a teenager, who is in rebellion to his parents' authority. The root of rebellion is witchcraft. A stiff-necked, defiant child can open a door into hell that allows curses and an aura of death in a family.

Another way witchcraft can enter a family is through music. Not all non-Christian music is categorically evil; however, there are some rock groups who are satanists and whose music in the hands of your teenager is a highway into hell. You must keep the standards God has given you for your home.

If you, as parents, react *without* prayer, the relationship with your child will be all the more given to the enemy! The outcome can often be curses levied against one another, sickness, and even death. But if you respond *with* prayer, with God's help the peace can be restored in your home and the devil expelled.

If we can successfully remove the witchcraft and the spread of curses from our relationships, we will find ourselves more fully secured in the stronghold of God.

Nay, in all these things we are more than
conquerors through him that loved us.

—ROMANS 8:37, KJV

16

"Oh, What God Has Done!"

True faith takes courage.

FOR ALL WE have spoken concerning principalities and powers, witchcraft and
curses, the most threatening battle we face
today is not in the spiritual realm; nor is it
on our streets or in our courts. Our greatest
battle is in our hearts: the fight of faith.

God is calling us to become "more than
conquerors" (Rom. 8:37, KJV). For those
who overcome, there will certainly be a
time when every good word God has ever
promised comes to pass. We will know and
experience God's stronghold on the highest
level; we will be instrumental in bringing
the divine antidote, the power of covenant

prayer with Christ, to remedy the ills of our world.

Until then, the Lord's immediate objective is to perfect faith in those whom He intends to use. However, true faith takes courage, for until the Word comes to pass in our lives, it will test us.

This is exactly where the church is today. We know we have heard from God; we are confident that revival is coming; and we have engaged in the work of intercession. Yet, apart from a few breakthroughs, the cities we have stood to defend are deteriorating morally and socially. These present tribulations are being accommodated by God as part of His plan to make the church in His image.

Paul said, "We also exult in our tribulations, knowing that tribulation brings about perseverance; and perseverance, proven character" (Rom. 5:3–4). The testing of our faith builds "proven character."

It is for this very reason that the test must, of necessity, take time; character is proven slowly. During this season God captures the heart and passion of His servants. Thus, the central question in the test of faith is, "Will we continue to believe God in spite of setbacks, duration of testing, or hostile circumstances?" The heart that continues to trust God through the tests demonstrates that the believer genuinely knows the true nature of God and that what God has promised He is also able to perform (Rom. 4:21).

Consider Joseph. Through a dream, the Lord revealed to Joseph that a time would come when he would rule over his family. Within days, however, these very brothers whom Joseph dreamed had bowed at his feet sold him into slavery!

The scriptural synopsis of Joseph's life gives us great insight into the ways of God toward His servants. It reads, "Until the time that his word came to pass, the word of the LORD tested him" (Ps. 105:19). The Word tests all God's servants before it is fulfilled.

Consider also Israel. God promised the Hebrews a land flowing with milk and honey. Their test of faith, however, immediately led them into a forty-year wilderness journey, full of setbacks and trials. One might question the validity of a promise that so many failed to attain. But for those who kept faith in God during the tests, everything the Lord promised came to pass.

The testimony of Joshua, who fully followed the Lord, was this: "Not one word of all the good words which the LORD . . . spoke concerning you has failed; all have been fulfilled for you" (Josh. 23:14). We must see that there will certainly be a time when "all the good words . . . have been fulfilled." Until then, the distance between our "Egypt" and "Canaan" is where our faith is being perfected.

A VISION OF THE HARVEST

SEVERAL YEARS AGO, RICK JOYNER'S BOOK *THE HARVEST* unlocked hope for tens of thousands of discouraged church leaders. Then, five years ago, John Dawson and I emerged, speaking essentially the same word: God wants our cities!

Though John and I were unknown to each other, he had named his book *Taking Our Cities for God,* which was also the title I was using for the conferences I was conducting.

For me, the hope of a national harvest began in 1971. In a night vision, the Lord showed me a city shrouded in terrible darkness, one similar to the blackness that descended upon Egypt. The darkness could be touched. I found myself outside the city. I was with people who had been purified, literally "baptized" in the glory of God. In the vision, I actually felt the power of God's glory, which was surging like brilliant bolts of lightning through us all. The vision ended with great multitudes leaving the darkness and surrendering their lives to Christ.

As I lay pondering the vision, I turned and opened my Bible; for the first time in my young Christian life, I read Isaiah 60.

> Arise, shine; for your light has come,
> and the glory of the LORD has risen
> upon you. For behold, darkness will
> cover the earth, and deep darkness
> the peoples; but the LORD will rise
> upon you, and His glory will appear
> upon you. And nations will come to
> your light, and kings to the bright-
> ness of your rising.
>
> —ISAIAH 60:1–3

This verse was confirmation to what I had seen in the vision! Darkness covered the earth, but the glory of the Lord had risen upon His people! In both the vision and the Scripture, multitudes were coming to the Lord out of darkness! Throughout my life, especially during times of testing and opposition, this vision of the harvest has been a great encouragement to me. However, it is upon the Scripture that my faith rests. Because of the Lord's promise from Isaiah 60, every time I see the darkness abounding, I know it is not a time to retreat but to arise and shine!

SCRIPTURE CANNOT BE BROKEN

I REST IN THE SCRIPTURE BECAUSE JESUS HIMSELF

said, "Scripture cannot be broken" (John 10:35). Do you understand this? *Scripture cannot be broken; it can only be fulfilled.* Jesus did not abolish the Law; He fulfilled it. Creation itself will pass away, but God's Word will have its fulfillment. Every promise God has made concerning His glory in the church, His wrath upon the nations, His purpose with Israel, and the harvest must have a fulfillment with people who hear, believe, and obtain the promise of God.

Fortunately for us, no matter what God purposes to do with mankind, He must, by necessity, start with imperfect people. God will supply virtue along the way, but what justifies us, even in our weaknesses, is our faith: We believe that what God has promised, He is able also to perform.

You see, God does not speak as a man in empty words or with wavering intentions. What proceeds from the mouth of God is the Son of God—the Word. He has all the attributes and power of God the Father. Because the Word is God, He cannot return to the Father without accomplishing all that heaven has purposed. God cannot fail.

Thus, if the Lord said His church will have "no spot or wrinkle or any such thing" (Eph. 5:27), Christ Himself guarantees that, although the Word is promised to imperfect people, it will be fulfilled. If the Lord says, "Greater works than [Mine] shall [you] do" (John 14:12), then that Word will certainly come to pass, no matter how weak the people are when they first believe God.

With God all things are possible. It is never a matter of *if* the Word will be fulfilled but *when* and *with whom,* for Scripture cannot be broken.

THE SHOUT OF A KING IS AMONG THEM!

YES, WE CAN POINT TO THE SINS AND FEARS THAT still reside in the church and excuse our faith from taking action. However, these flaws could also describe the Israelites the night they left Egypt. In spite of their sinful condition, God fulfilled His promises. He delivered Israel out of its bondage to sin and fear. In the relatively short period of forty years, the Lord transformed a nation that had known only slavery for hundreds of years; He made them into a mighty army, feared by all nations.

Therefore, let us consider Israel after the wilderness, now on the plains of Midian, about to enter the Promised Land. Note that just before Israel entered Canaan, Balak, the Midianite king, sought to stop them with witchcraft. Yet, every time the sorcerer Balaam began to curse, blessings poured forth instead. Balaam said, "How shall I curse, whom God has not cursed? And how can I denounce, whom the LORD has not denounced?" (Num. 23:8).

As we stated earlier, there is no power in the universe except what comes from God. In His relationship with man, God's power manifests in either His blessing or His curse. While the blessing of God abounds in our world and can be seen in the abundance and beauty of creation, Paul tells us God's wrath abides upon "ungodliness and unrighteousness" (Rom. 1:18).

Satan is not a deity with power to create good and evil. He is a fallen angel, imprisoned by divine decree in darkness (Jude 6). Satan's cunning is that he is able to manipulate the darkness in which he is trapped and, in a limited way, serve his own will. However, the influence of hell, its powers and curses, is confined to what is already under divine judgment. Thus, Pharaoh's sorcerers seemingly could reproduce the plagues of Moses because the plagues were originally the judgments of God.

The entry point through which a curse finds access to an individual's life is sin. If we are free from sin, no curse can attach itself to us, for a curse cannot penetrate what God has blessed. Thus, Balaam said, "There is no sorcery against Jacob, nor is there any divination against Israel." Why? "He has not observed iniquity in Jacob. He has blessed and I cannot revoke it." (See Numbers 23.)

God brought Israel to the place of spiritual immunity to Balaam's curses. This is an amazing statement! Are not these the sons and daughters of those who, because of their disobedience and unbelief, died in the wilderness? Yes, but God changed them! Although Balaam was a sorcerer, he was more familiar with the integrity of God's promise than most Christians! He declared to Balak:

> Arise, O Balak, and hear . . . God is not a man, that He should lie, nor a son of man, that He should repent; has He said, and will He not do it? Or has He spoken, and will He not make it good?
> —Numbers 23:18–19

The Lord promised Israel He would deliver them from Egypt if they would worship Him in the wilderness and then go in to take Canaan. Balaam said, "The God of Israel has done exactly what He promised!"

During the long wilderness years, we can imagine that there were many rumors among the nations concerning Israel: "What is the God of the Hebrews doing?" Many negative things must have been said. Even among the Hebrews, opinions were bad: "You brought us into the wilderness to kill us because there weren't enough graves in Egypt."

Yet, Balaam tells us that the questions and comments about Israel all changed. Remember, this is the report of hell's view of the people of God! Balaam observes:

> The LORD his God is with him, and the shout of a King is among them. God brings them out of Egypt; He has strength like a wild ox . . . It now must be said of Jacob and of Israel, "Oh, what God has done!"
> —NUMBERS 23:21–23, NKJV

Whatever was said negatively in the past about Israel became mere history. Now, "the Lord is with them!"

Remember: At this time Israel had no human king. But now, as Balaam attunes himself to the spiritual realm, he hears the shout, the "war cry," of the Lord of Hosts! He says, "The shout of a king is among them." The true King of Israel had aligned His power with Israel's armies! God delivered them from Egypt; God prepared them in the wilderness! For all the former criticisms and comments, now the only thing that comes to mind when the nations see Israel is, "Oh, what God has done!"

So it shall be with the praying, persevering church. There will certainly be a time when the tests are over and our character proven. It shall then be said among the nations: "Oh, what God has done! How the Almighty changed these men and women! How He took the foolish, weak, and base things of this world to nullify the way things were! Are these not the same people who were once full of sin and fear? Yet now they are one people, united and baptized in the glory of God! Behold! The shout of their King is with them; the war cry of the archangel goes before them."

And it will happen, because God is not a man that He should lie. It has been written, and it cannot be broken. If God said it, He will do it. If He spoke it, He will make it good. The day will come when heaven and earth, yes, and even hell, will gaze upon the church and say, *"Oh, what God has done!"*

Other Books by Francis Frangipane

The Three Battlegrounds
(hardback and paperback versions)

Holiness, Truth and the
Presence of God

The Days of His Presence

The River of Life

The House of the Lord

For more information on the ministry of
Francis Frangipane, contact:

Arrow Publications
P.O. Box 10102
Cedar Rapids, IA 52410-0102

Phone: (319) 373-3011
Fax: (319) 373-3012